THE COMPLETE MERDE!

THE COMPLETE MERDE!

GENEVIÈVE

Illustrated by
MICHAEL HEATH

*The REAL French You Were
Never Taught At School*

HarperCollins*Publishers*

HarperCollins*Publishers*
77–85 Fulham Palace Road,
Hammersmith, London W6 8JB

This paperback edition 1996
9 8

MERDE! first published in Great Britain by
Angus and Robertson UK 1984
Previously published by Fontana 1991
Reprinted twice
Published by HarperCollins 1995

MERDE ENCORE! first published in Great Britain by
Angus and Robertson UK 1986
Published by Fontana 1991

ISBN 0 00 255768 1

Printed in Great Britain by
Clays Ltd, St Ives plc

CONTENTS

Merde! vii
Merde Encore! 83

MERDE!

A mes vieux (René et Nanette)
A mon frangin (Hervé)
A mon mec (Richard)
A mes gosses (Rupert, Oliver et Jamyn)

CONTENTS

PREFACE   xiii
  Guidance   xiii

I THE MUSTS   1
  Common Everyday Musts   1
  The Absolute Musts   10
    The MERDE Family   10
    The CHIER Family   14
    The CON Family   15
    The FICHER and FOUTRE Families   16

II VARIATIONS ON A THEME   21
  Theme One: What an Idiot   21
  Theme Two: What a Pain   23
  Theme Three: I Don't Give a Damn   25

III THE BODY AND ITS FUNCTIONS   27
  The Parts   27
  Bodily Functions   30
  Body Types   34

IV THE WEIGHTY MATTERS OF LOVE AND SEX
(NATIONAL OBSESSION NUMBER ONE)   39
  The Protagonists   39
  The Chase   44
  Emotions and Conquest   45
  Parties   48
  Disasters   50

V THE NO LESS WEIGHTY MATTERS OF FOOD AND
DRINK (NATIONAL OBSESSION NUMBER TWO)   54
  Food   54
  Drink   56

VI AGGRO   60

VII MONEY MATTERS   65

VIII WORK AND SOCIAL STATUS   67
   Work and Jobs   67
   Social Status and Political Affiliation   69

IX INDULGING IN RACISM, XENOPHOBIA AND
DISRESPECT FOR ONE'S ELDERS   72

X TO EXIT RAPIDLY   75

XI POSITIVE THINKING   76

XII FOREIGN INVASIONS OF THE LANGUAGE   78

XIII YOUR FINAL EXAM   81

PREFACE

Do you remember when you were learning French at school and looked in vain through your dictionary for all the dirty words? Have you thought you had a reasonable command of the language, then seen a French film or gone to France, only to find that you could barely understand a word? You were, of course, never taught *real* French by your boring teachers who failed to give you the necessary tools of communication while stuffing the subjunctive imperfect down your throat. French "argot" (slang) is not just the dirty words (though, have no fear, you will find them here), it is an immensely rich language with its own words for very ordinary things, words that are in constant use. Here, then, is not an exhaustive or scholarly dictionary of "argot" (that would be ten times thicker) but a guide to survival in understanding everyday French as it is *really* spoken.

Guidance

Asterisks after "argot" words indicate a degree of rudeness above the ordinary colloquial. Two asterisks show a whopper, although you should not assume that strength and rudeness cause a word to be used less frequently, "au contraire" . . .

When an English definition is underlined, that definition gives a good equivalent flavour, feeling and degree of rudeness of the French word. Good equivalents are not that common, so rely generally on the English definition for the meaning of the French word, on the asterisks for its strength and on the many examples for its usage. Just remember, to be authentic is to be rude.

I THE MUSTS

Common Everyday Musts

So many everyday words have their colloquial counterparts which appear constantly in conversation. The following is a list of the most frequently used and, therefore, most necessary ones, which do not fall into any of the neat categories of subsequent sections.

NECESSARY NOUNS

People

a fellow, a guy, a man	un type
	un gars
	un mec*
a woman	une bonne femme*
a bird, a chick, a broad	une gonzesse**
a kid	un/une môme
	un/une gosse
	un gamin, une gamine
what's-his-name	machin, machin-chouette
what's-her-name	machine, machine-chouette
a friend	un copain, une copine
Mrs, Miss, ma	la mère (la mère Dupont a dit = ma Dupont said)
Mr, pa, old man	le père (le père Dupont = old man Dupont)
parents	les vieux

the old man (father)	le paternel le vieux
the old lady (mother)	la maternelle la vieille
a son	un fiston
son! young man! junior! (USA)	fiston!
a brother	un frangin
a sister	une frangine
a beastly person	un chameau (literally, a camel)

a bastard	un salaud** (ce salaud de Dupont = that bastard Dupont) un salopard**
a bitch	une salope** (cette salope de Marie = that bitch Marie)
a bastard or a bitch	une vache* (literally, a cow) une peau de vache* (literally, a cow's hide)
a shit	un fumier* (literally, manure)
an arse-licker	un lèche-cul**
a boot-licker	un lèche-bottes*

Animals

a dog, a mutt (USA)	un cabot* un klebs* un klébard*
a bird	un piaf* (remember Edith Piaf?)

Things

nothing	quedale, or que dalle
a book	un bouquin
a car	une bagnole
an old banger	un tacot
a slow vehicle	un veau (literally, a calf)
a fag (the one you smoke)	une sèche
water	la flotte
paper	du papelard
a rag (newspaper)	une feuille de chou (literally, a cabbage leaf) un canard

3

a <u>bike</u>	une bécane
	un vélo
a <u>pad</u> (room)	une piaule
the <u>sack</u> (bed)	le pieu
	le plumard (from "la plume" = the feather)
a lamp	une loupiote
the <u>telly</u>, the <u>box</u>	la télé
a phone call	un coup de fil
a boat	un rafiot
a thing, a <u>thingummyjig</u>	un bidule
	un truc
	un machin
	un fourbi
	un engin
the <u>loo</u>, the <u>can</u> (USA)	les water (from "les WC" = the water-closet)
	les chiottes**
a snag	un pépin
a mess, a shambles	la pagaille, la pagaïe
a <u>balls-up</u>, a mess	un bordel**

Clothes

clothes	les frusques (m.)
	les fringues (f.)
	les nippes (f.)
a hat	un bitos
	un galurin
a suit	un costard
a pair of trousers	un falzar
a shirt	une liquette

4

a raincoat	un imper (short for "un imperméable)
shoes	les godasses (f.) les pompes (f.) les tatanes (f.)
outsize shoes	les écrase-merde** (f.) (literally, shit-squashers)
an umbrella	un pépin un pébroque
a ring	une bagouse
a suitcase	une valoche

NECESSARY ADJECTIVES

friendly and nice	sympa (short for "sympathique")
exhausting	crevant,e
killingly funny	crevant,e tordant,e
funny	rigolo, rigolote
disgusting	dégueulasse* débectant,e* (from "débecter*" = to puke)
ugly; lousy	moche
useless, no good	à la gommé à la noix

NECESSARY VERBS

to understand	piger
to not understand a damn thing about	ne piger quedale à

5

to <u>dig up</u>, to find	dégoter, dégotter
to lose	paumer
to watch out for, to be careful about	faire gaffe à
to make a mistake	faire une gaffe (note the difference from the preceding expression) se gourer
to <u>bust</u>	bousiller péter*
to have some nerve, to be cheeky	avoir du culot être culotté,e avoir du toupet être gonflé,e (literally, to be swollen)
to go too far, to push things	charrier

6

to be an enthusiast, to be crazy (about)	être un fana, une fana ("fana" is short for "fanatique"; c'est un fana de la voile = he's crazy about sailing)
to have a good time, to laugh	rigoler se marrer
to kid, to joke	rigoler (tu rigoles, non? = are you kidding?)
to grouse	rouspéter (gives "un rouspéteur, une rouspéteuse" = a moaner, grumbler) râler (gives "un râleur, une râleuse" = a moaner, grumbler)
to be in a good mood	être de bon poil être bien vissé,e (literally, to be well screwed in) être bien luné,e
to be in a bad mood	être de mauvais poil être mal vissé,e être mal luné,e
to not make much of an effort	ne pas se fouler
to be lucky	avoir du bol avoir du pot
to be unlucky	manquer de bol manquer de pot
to nick, to pinch (to steal)	chiper pincer piquer faucher barboter rafler
to lick someone's boots	faire de la lèche à quelqu'un*
to be pouring with rain	flotter

7

to be landed with	se farcir*

NECESSARY BITS AND PIECES

yes	ouais
OK	d'ac (short for "d'accord")
no way!	des clous! tintin!
so what?	et alors? ben quoi? (ben = eh bien)
damn!	zut! la barbe!
goddammit! oh my God!	putain**! (literally, whore)
that damn ..., that bloody ...	ce putain de ..., cette putaine de ...**
you ...	espèce de ... (espèce de salaud = you bastard)
you ... (pl.)	bande de ... (bande d'idiots = you bunch of idiots)
extremely + an adjective	archi- (archi-dégueulasse = extremely disgusting)
very, really	vachement drôlement rudement
shut up!	écrase*! ferme-la*! ta gueule**! ("gueule" is literally an animal's mouth, but is used pejoratively for people's mouths or faces)
I dare you!	chiche!

my arse!	mon cul**!
hi!	salut!
this afternoon	c't'aprèm (short for "cet après-midi)
what? huh?	hein?
phew!	ouf!
ow, ouch!	aie! ouille!
yuk!	beurk!

A FEW TIPS FOR CONSTRUCTING AUTHENTIC-SOUNDING SENTENCES

- Clip the end vowel off pronouns. Say "t'es sympa" instead of "tu es sympa".

- "Ce," "cet," and "cette" are clipped to become "c'", "c't" and "c'te". Say "c'mec" (pronounced "smec") instead of "ce mec".

- Use "y'a" for "il y a" and "y'avait" for "il y avait".

- Omit the "ne" from the negative "ne ... pas". Say "j'sais pas" (pronounced "chais pas") instead of "je ne sais pas".

- Emphasise the subject by adding the relevant indirect pronoun at the end of the sentence. Say "j'sais pas, moi", "t'as du pot, toi". Or stress the subject by adding the noun that a subject pronoun connotes. Say "elles sont moches, ces godasses", "il est gonflé, c'mec".

NOW TRY YOUR HAND AT THE FOLLOWING SENTENCES

1 C't'espèce de salaud de frangin de Jojo m'a piqué ma bécane. Il a du toupet, c'mec.

2 "Passe-moi un coup de fil c't'aprèm." "D'ac."

3 Oh, putain, j'ai bousillé la bagnole du paternel.

4 Ton copain est vachement sympa, hein?

5   Aie! Fais gaffe, tu m'fais mal!

6   Il est pas rigolo, le gars. Il est toujours de mauvais poil.

7   J'pige quedale à c'bouquin, moi.

8   Allez, venez, les gars, à la flotte!

9   C'est moche; la mère machine-chouette a paumé son cabot.

10 Où est-ce que t'as dégotté c'truc dégueulasse?

11 Tu charries, ta piaule est un vrai bordel.

1   That Jojo's bastard of a brother has nicked my bike. That guy has got some nerve.

2   "Give me a ring this afternoon." "OK."

3   Oh, hell, I've busted my old man's car.

4   Your friend is really nice, isn't he?

5   Ouch! Watch it, you're hurting me!

6   That fellow isn't much fun. He's always in a bad mood.

7   I don't get a damn thing about this book.

8   Hey, come on fellows, let's jump in (that is, in the water)!

9   It's too bad; old ma what's-her-name has lost her dog.

10 Where did you find that disgusting thing?

11 It's a bit much, your room is a real mess.

The Absolute Musts

The MERDE** Family

"Merde**" means literally and figuratively "shit". It is known in polite circles as "les cinq lettres" (as we would say "a four-letter word"). But then, there are few such circles, and the word is vital for communication with the natives. It does not have the impact and shock value of its English equivalent, so sprinkle liberally. The "merde**" family has several nominal, adjectival and verbal forms, so it can be, and is, handily inserted anywhere and anyhow.

NOUNS

la merde** = the <u>shit</u>
as in:

J'ai marché dans de la merde**.
I walked in some <u>dogshit</u>.

Oh, merde** alors!
Oh, shit! Oh, hell! Oh, damn!

and in the expressions:

être dans la merde**
<u>to be up shit creek</u>

se foutre** dans la merde**
to get it all wrong (literally, to put oneself in the shit)

ne pas se prendre pour de la petite merde**
to take oneself very seriously, to think oneself great (literally, to not take oneself for small shit)

un emmerdement** = a real problem, trouble

J'ai des emmerdements** avec ma bagnole.
I'm having real trouble with my car.

un emmerdeur, une emmerdeuse** = a pain in the neck

Ce type est un emmerdeur** de premier ordre.
That fellow is a first-class pain in the neck.

le merdier** = a fine mess, a jam, a fix (literally, the shitpile)

T'es dans un de ces merdiers**, toi alors!
You sure are in a fine mess!

un petit merdeux, une petite merdeuse** = a little twerp

Le môme du père Dupont est un vrai petit merdeux**.
Old man Dupont's kid is a real little twerp.

un démerdeur, une démerdeuse** = one who always manages,
one who always gets what he/she wants (literally, one who always
gets out of the shit)

J'ai jamais vu une démerdeuse** comme Pascale.
I've never known anyone always to get her own way like
Pascale.

la démerde** = the art of being resourceful, of always landing on
one's feet, of always getting what one wants (the French do
consider this, known also as "le système D", an art form)

Ce mec* est un champion de la démerde**.
This fellow is a master at landing on his feet.

merde! = good luck! (before a challenge, such as an exam)

Bon, allez, merde, ça ira!
Well, good luck, it'll be OK!

ADJECTIVES

emmerdant,e** = annoying, irritating, boring, a <u>pain in the neck</u>

Qu'est-ce qu'il est emmerdant** ton frangin!
What a pain your brother is!

emmerdé,e** = worried, annoyed

12

J'suis drôlement emmerdé**, j'ai paumé mon imper.
I'm really annoyed, I've lost my raincoat.

VERBS

emmerder** = to annoy, to irritate, to <u>give someone a pain in the neck</u>

> Elle m'emmerde** cette bonne femme*, elle n'arrête pas de râler.
> That woman gets on my nerves, she never stops complaining.

and in the expression:

> **Je l'emmerde****, **je les emmerde****.
> To hell with him/her, to hell with them.

s'emmerder** = to be bored stiff

> Qu'est-ce qu'on s'emmerde** ici.
> What a bore it is here.

se démerder** = to manage, to get by

> Ma copine se démerde** toujours pour avoir les meilleures places.
> My girlfriend always manages to get the best seats.

The CHIER** Family

Anal matters again! Draw your own conclusions about their importance in the French language and psyche. "Chier**" means literally "to crap". The family of words derives from this meaning but has expanded to express intense annoyance and irritation. "Chiant**", for example, is one step further in rudeness than "emmerdant**", as "pain in the arse" is stronger than "pain in the neck".

VERBS

chier** = to <u>crap</u>

> Son sale cabot a chié** partout dans ma piaule.
> Her rotten old dog crapped all over my room.

faire chier** = to <u>give a real pain in the arse</u>

> Ma maternelle me fait chier**.
> My mother gives me a real pain in the arse.

envoyer chier quelqu'un** = to tell someone to fuck off

> Un de ces jours, je vais envoyer mon vieux chier**.
> One of these days I'm going to tell my old man to fuck off.

NOUNS

la chiasse** = the runs, and thence, fear

> Rien que de penser aux examens, il a la chiasse**.
> Just thinking about exams gives him the runs.

les chiottes** (f.) = the bog (UK), the can (USA)

> C'est par là, les chiottes**?
> Is the bog that way?

une chierie** = a whole mess of problems; a drag

> Quelle chierie**, l'école!
> What a drag school is!

ADJECTIVE

chiant,e** = extremely irritating, boring, a <u>pain in the arse</u>

14

Elle est chiante**, cette môme.
That kid is a real pain in the arse.

C'est chiant**, ça.
That's a real drag.

The CON** Family

Physically, we haven't moved too far away, as we reach the third
absolutely vital must. "Con**" means literally "cunt", but is used
constantly and emphatically to indicate stupidity, thickness, some-
what as Americans use "asshole". As with "merde" and "chier",
"con**" is everywhere in conversation and gives rise to a family of
words.

NOUNS

un con, un connard**
une conne, une connasse, une connarde** = an idiot, a jerk, a fool

Quel con**, ce mec*!
What a damn fool that fellow is!

une connerie** = a stupidity; rubbish

Ma frangine ne fait que des conneries**.
My sister does nothing but stupid things.

C'est de la vraie connerie**, ce bouquin.
This book is a load of rubbish.

ADJECTIVES

con, conne**
connard, connarde** = stupid, thick, dumb

Les filles sont connes**.
Girls are real idiots.

Il a l'air con**.
He looks stupid.

VERBS

déconner** = to fool about; to do foolish things; to talk rubbish

Hé, les gosses, vous avez fini de déconner**?
Hey, kids, have you finished fooling about?

Ce machin déconne**.
This thing is going bonkers.

faire le con** = to act stupidly

Faut toujours qu'il fasse le con**, ce mec*.
That fellow can never act sensibly.

The FICHER* and FOUTRE** Families

The verbs "ficher*" and "foutre**" are very useful and necessary:
they can mean "to do", "to give", "to put", and they figure in
many vivid expressions. "Foutre**" is the stronger of the two.
Learn their usage through these examples; for the sake of easy
reading, only "foutre**" will be used but, remember, either verb
works.

VERBS

foutre** = to do
ne rien foutre** = to not do a damn thing

Qu'est-ce que tu fous**?
What the hell are you doing?

Mon frangin ne fout** rien en classe.
My brother doesn't do a damn thing in class.

foutre** **une baffe** = to give a slap

Arrête ou je te fous** une baffe.
Quit it or I'll slap you.

foutre** **la paix à quelqu'un** = to leave someone alone

Foutez-nous** la paix!
Leave us alone!

foutre** **la trouille à quelqu'un** = to scare the hell out of someone

Ce klebs* a l'air enragé: il me fout** la trouille.
This dog looks rabid: it scares the hell out of me.

foutre** = to put

16

Où as-tu foutu** les clefs de la maison?
Where the hell did you put the house keys?

foutre le camp** = to push off, to get the hell out

Allez, foutez-moi** le camp d'ici, bande de voyous.
Go on, push off, you hooligans.

Hé, les gars, foutons** le camp avant que les flics n'arrivent.
Hey, you guys, let's push off before the fuzz comes.

foutre au panier** = to bung in the waste paper basket, to <u>chuck out</u>

Un de ces jours, j'vais foutre** la télé au panier.
One of these days I'm going to chuck the telly out.

foutre en l'air** = to <u>chuck out</u>, to ruin

La maternelle a foutu** toutes mes vieilles godasses en l'air.
My mother chucked all my old shoes out.

Le mauvais temps a foutu** tous nos plans en l'air.
The bad weather ruined all our plans.

foutre à la porte** = to kick out; to sack

Ses vieux l'ont foutu** à la porte.
His parents kicked him out of the house.

Son patron l'a foutu** à la porte.
His boss sacked him.

se foutre de quelqu'un** = to take the mickey out of someone, to make fun of someone; to take someone for a ride, to rip someone off

Mes copains se sont foutus** de mon falzar.
My friends made fun of my trousers.

Il s'est foutu** de toi le mec* qui t'a vendu cette bagnole.
The fellow who sold you this car took you for a ride.

se foutre de la gueule** des gens, se foutre** de la poire* du monde** = to take everyone for a damn idiot

Quoi, quinze francs pour un café? Vous vous foutez** de la gueule** des gens, non?
What, fifteen francs for a cup of coffee? You've got to be kidding!

s'en foutre** **de** = to not give a damn about

> Je m'en fous** de ce que tu en penses.
> I don't give a damn what you think about it.

se foutre** **dedans** = to make a real mess (of something), to make a mistake

> Cette fois-ci, il s'est vraiment foutu** dedans.
> This time he really put his foot in it.
> (The French and the English expressions both imply stepping into something nasty.)

se foutre** **parterre** = to fall flat on one's face

> Fais gaffe, tu vas te foutre** parterre!
> Watch it, you're going to fall flat on your face!

The following two expressions are used only as given here:

Ça la fout** **mal** = It's a damned awkward situation.

Va te/Allez vous faire foutre**! = <u>Piss off! Fuck off! Get stuffed!</u>

The participles "**fichu,e***" and "**foutu,e****" can also mean "done for", "finished", "ruined".

> La télé est foutue**.
> The telly has had it.

ADJECTIVES

The adjectival forms, "fichu,e*" and "foutu,e**", are used in the following expressions:

être mal foutu,e** = to feel rotten, ill; to work badly, to be badly set up

> J'vais pas en classe aujourd'hui, j'suis mal foutu**.
> I'm not going to school today, I feel lousy.

> Ce magasin est mal foutu**.
> This shop is badly laid out.

être bien foutu,e** = to have a great body; to work well, to be well set up

> Elle est vachement bien foutue**, ta frangine.
> Your sister sure has a great body.

> Cette bagnole est drôlement bien foutue**.
> This car is really nifty.

être foutu,e** de faire quelque chose = to be liable to do something

> Fais gaffe, il est foutu** de tout bousiller.
> Watch it, he's liable to bust everything.

ne même pas être foutu,e** de faire quelque chose = to not even be capable of doing something, to not even be willing to do something

> Il n'est même pas foutu** de lui envoyer une carte pour son anniversaire.
> He can't even be bothered to send her a card for her birthday.

"**Fichu,e***" and "**foutu,e****" are used as "damned", "bloody", etc.

> Ce foutu** temps est déprimant.
> This bloody weather is depressing.

19

NOUNS

Two nouns belong to the foutre** family only:

le foutoir** = a shambles, a mess

Ta piaule est un vrai foutoir**
Your room is a real mess.

la foutaise** = a load of old rubbish

C'est de la foutaise**, ton truc.
That thing of yours is a load of old rubbish.

II VARIATIONS ON A THEME

Fact: the French individual feels superior to his fellow man, foreign or not. Consequence: the French have a very wide selection of words to express their contempt for the intellectual, mental or spiritual inferiority of others as well as their annoyance derived from this contempt. The two following sections give you the range of words to which you might be subjected. The third offers a few replies.

Theme One: What an Idiot

a jerk, an idiot, a fool

un con, une conne**,
  un connard, une connarde**,
  une connasse** (remember chapter I?)
un couillon** (from "les couilles**" (f.) = testicles)

crazy, <u>cracked</u>, <u>bonkers</u>, <u>nuts</u>

dingue
dingo
cinglé,e
zinzin
timbré,e
sonné,e
siphonné,e
tapé,e
piqué,e
toqué,e
maboul,e
loufoque
marteau
malade

21

All these and the following adjectives except "marteau" can be used as nouns when preceded by an article. For example,

C'est un vrai cinglé, ce type.
That fellow is a real nutcase.

Où as-tu dégotté une dingue pareille?
Where did you pick up such a crazy woman?

half-witted, mentally defective	débile demeuré,e arriéré,e crétin,e
a half-wit, a mental defective	un débile mental, une débile mentale un minus
degenerate	dégénéré,e taré,e
dim	paumé,e (remember "paumer" = to lose)
a clot, a twit	une andouille un corniaud une cruche une gourde un pied une patate
a nitwit	un ballot
silly	bébête cucul* (cucul la praline* = silly billy)
a silly goose	une bécasse
thick, dumb	con, conne** bouché,e
gaga , senile	gaga gâteux, gâteuse
weird	tordu,e

22

a scatterbrain	une tête de linotte
to go off one's rocker, to go round the twist	dérailler (literally, to go off the rails) débloquer ne pas tourner rond
to have a screw loose	avoir une case de vide, (literally, to have an empty compartment) être tombé,e sur le crâne (literally, to have fallen on one's skull)
to be as thick as two posts	être con comme un balai** être con comme la lune* (this particular "lune" being not the moon, but the backside)
are you crazy?	ça va pas, non?

To lessen the offensiveness of a term, you can use "un peu ... sur les bords". For example,

Elle est un peu zinzin sur les bords.
She's a bit on the cracked side (literally, she's a bit cracked around the edges).

Theme Two: What a Pain

He/she is a real pain	Il/elle est casse-pieds Il/elle est emmerdant,e** Il/elle est chiant,e**
irritating	enquiquinant,e empoisonnant,e
boring	barbant,e rasant,e rasoir
to bore	barber raser (literally, to shave, and the

shaving imagery to indicate boredom gives rise to an important gesture that you should be able to interpret. If you see a Frenchman raise his arm and stroke his cheek with the back of his fingers, you will know that he is indicating his boredom and irritation with a person or a situation.)

deadly boring	assommant,e (assommer = to knock out)
to get on someone's nerves	taper quelqu'un sur les nerfs casser les pieds de quelqu'un les casser à quelqu'un (the "les" can refer to "pieds" or "couilles**")
to <u>give someone a pain in the neck, arse; to piss someone off</u>	faire suer quelqu'un (suer = perspire) faire chier quelqu'un** emmerder quelqu'un**
to irritate	enquiquiner empoisonner
to be fed up with	en avoir marre de en avoir plein le dos de en avoir ras le bol de en avoir plein le cul de**
<u>What a drag</u>!	quelle barbe!
to not be able to stand someone	ne pas pouvoir sentir quelqu'un ne pas pouvoir piffer quelqu'un* ne pas pouvoir blairer quelqu'un* ("le pif*" and "le blair*" mean the <u>conk</u>. These three expressions therefore literally mean "not to be able to smell someone," reminding us of the prominence of French noses.)

to not be able to stand someone	ne pas pouvoir voir quelqu'un
	ne pas pouvoir voir quelqu'un en peinture
	ne pas pouvoir encaisser quelqu'un
to disgust	débecter*

Theme Three: I Don't Give a Damn

I don't give a damn	je m'en fiche*
	je m'en fous**
	je m'en contrefiche*
	je m'en contrefous**
	je m'en balance*
	je m'en bats l'oeil*

I don't give a fuck	je m'en branle** (branler** = to masturbate; this expression is rather strong!)

To say that you don't give a damn about a certain thing, use any of the above followed by "de" and the object of your indifference. For example,

Je m'en fous de ton programme de télé, finis tes devoirs d'abord.
I don't give a damn about your TV programme, finish your homework first.

REVISION

Just a few sentences to see if you have absorbed the previous vocabulary.

1 Une gonzesse plutôt conne sortait avec un mec vachement sympa. Mais le type commençait à en avoir marre d'elle parce qu'elle pigeait jamais rien. Un jour, il en avait vraiment ras le bol. Il lui a dit de foutre le camp. "T'as du toupet," dit-elle, en lui foutant une baffe. La garce a appelé son cabot, en plus, pour déchirer le falzar du gars, ce qui l'a vraiment fait chier. "Salope!" cria-t-il, "Va te faire foutre!"

2 Je peux pas blairer ce débile de Jojo. Il emmerde le monde avec tous ses problèmes.

3 Les anglais sont complètement dingues, ils conduisent leurs bagnoles du mauvais côté.

4 C'est toujours les plus cons qui se prennent pas pour de la petite merde.

1 A pretty thick woman was going out with some really nice guy. But the fellow was beginning to get fed up with her because she never understood anything. One day, he'd really had it. He told her to push off. "You've got a cheek," she said, slapping him. What's more, the cow called her dog to tear the guy's trousers, which really pissed him off. "You bitch!" he yelled, "Fuck off!"

2 I can't stand that half-wit Jojo. He bugs everyone with all his problems.

3 The English are really crazy, they drive their cars on the wrong side.

4 It's always the dumbest who think they're so great.

Now, if you have mastered the previous chapters, we can begin to have fun, what with the body and sex coming up.

III THE BODY AND ITS FUNCTIONS

The Parts

the body	la carcasse (mainly in the expression "bouge ta carcasse" = budge, move!)
the head	le caillou (particularly in the expression "pas un poil sur le caillou" = as bald as a coot, literally, not a hair on the stone) le crâne (literally, the skull)
the <u>nut</u>	la citrouille (literally, the pumpkin)
the brain, the head	le ciboulot
the brain	les méninges (mainly in the expression "se creuser les méninges" = to rack one's brain)
the <u>mug</u> , the face	la gueule** la tronche* la bouille la trogne*
hair	les tifs (m.)
the <u>conk</u>, the nose	le pif* le blair*
the eyes	les mirettes (f.)
the ears	les esgourdes (f.)

27

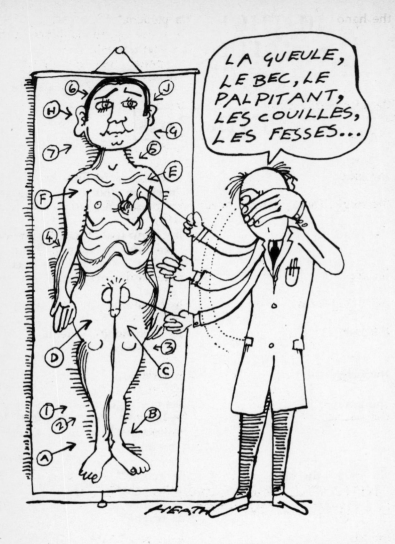

the mouth	le bec* (literally, the beak)
	la gueule**
the lips	les babines (f.)
the moustache	les bacchantes (f.)
the beard	la barbouze

the hand	la paluche*
	la pince (serrer la pince = to shake hands)
	la patte* (bas les pattes* = hands off)
the biceps (muscles)	les biscoteaux (m.)
the leg	la patte*
	la guibole*
the pins	les quilles* (f.)
the thighs (heavy female ones)	les jambons* (m.; literally, the hams)
	les gigots* (m.; literally, the legs of lamb)
the foot	le panard*
the ticker (heart)	le palpitant
the guts	les boyaux* (m.)
	les tripes* (f.)
the belly	le bide*
	le bidon*
the paunch	la bedaine
	la brioche

AND NOW THOSE WORDS YOU'VE BEEN LOOKING ALL OVER FOR

the tits	les nichons* (m.)
	les miches* (f.)
	les tétons* (m.)
	les doudounes* (f.)
the genital organ, male or female	le zizi (a word used from early childhood onwards)
the dick	la kiquette*, la quéquette*

the cock	la bitte**
	la queue** (literally, the tail)
	la verge** (literally, the rod)
	le zob**
	la pine**
the balls	les couilles** (f.)
the family jewels	les bijoux de famille
the pussy	le chat*
	la chatte*
	le con**
the clit	la praline* ("praline" is a sugared almond and the use of the word for clit comes from the similarity in shape)
the bottom, the bum, the backside	l'arrière-train
	les fesses* (f.; a useful expression to describe others, not yourself, is "avoir le feu aux fesses*" = to be in a hurry)
	le derche
the arse	la lune*
	le cul** ("le papier-cul**" or "pécu**" from the initial "p" for "papier" + "cul**" = toilet paper, bogroll)
the rump	la croupe*
the arsehole	le trou de balle**

Bodily Functions

to cry	chialer*
to be tired	être crevé,e
	être vanné,e

LE BEAU CHAT

to be <u>washed out</u>	être lessivé,e (la lessive = the washing)
to sleep	roupiller pioncer
to take a catnap	pousser un roupillon
to <u>be dying of cold, heat, hunger, thirst</u>	crever de froid, de chaud, de faim, de soif

31

to be cold	cailler (as in "je caille" = I'm freezing)
to catch a cold	attraper la crève
to be ill	avoir la crève
to <u>puke</u>	dégobiller* dégueuler**
to grow old, to <u>be getting on</u>	prendre de la bouteille prendre du bouchon
to <u>kick the bucket</u>, to <u>snuff it</u>, to die	crever* (note the versatility of the word which literally means "to burst" and make sure you learn the variations of use above as they do make for variations of meaning) caner* claquer* clamecer* casser sa pipe
a <u>stiff</u> (corpse)	un macchabée, un macab*
to <u>stink</u> (applied only to living creatures)	puer le bouc (literally, to smell of goat) puer le fauve (literally, to smell of wild animal)
to <u>stink</u> (generally applicable)	puer cocoter* fouetter* schlinguer*
to burp	roter
to <u>piss</u>	pisser* faire pipi (the childish term)
to <u>crap</u>	chier** faire caca (the childish term)
to <u>wipe one's arse</u>	se torcher le cul**

32

shit	la merde**
turds	les étrons (m.)
to fart	péter* (this verb gives rise to a few useful expressions: péter plus haut que son cul** = to think too highly of oneself; literally, to fart higher than one's arse péter le feu* = to be full of energy; literally, to fart fire un pète-sec* = a strict disciplinarian; literally, a clean, dry farter

a fart	un pet*
to have a hard-on	bander** avoir la tringle**
to jerk oneself off, to masturbate	se branler** se tripoter*

Body Types

to be striking	avoir de la gueule
a handsome young thing (male)	un beau gosse
to be well endowed (both sexes)	être bien monté,e
naked	à poil
a beanpole (both sexes)	une grande asperge une grande bringue une grande perche
a puny runt	un avorton** (literally, the left-over from an abortion) un résidu de fausse couche** (literally, the leftover from a miscarriage)
a midget	un nabot
a skinny bones	un maigrichon, une maigrichonne
as thin as a rake	maigre comme un clou
a hulking great brute	une armoire à glace (literally, a wardrobe) un balaise un malabar
big, large	mastoc maousse

34

brawny, well-built	baraqué,e
a big, tough guy	un casseur (literally, one who breaks things)
a big woman, a <u>horse</u>	un grand cheval une jument (literally, a mare)
a dumpy little woman	un pot à tabac (literally, a tobacco pot)
a really ugly, stubby woman, a <u>dog</u>	un boudin* (literally, black pudding, a stubby sausage)
mannish (said of a woman)	hommasse
a <u>big fatso</u>	un gros patapouf un gros plein de soupe
a <u>fat slob</u>	un gros lard
to have big tits	avoir du monde au balcon
to <u>be well rounded</u>	être bien roulée être bien balancée être bien carrossée (la carrosserie = the car body)
a handsome morsel	un beau morceau
to be flat-chested	être plate comme une limande (la limande = the sole) être plate comme une planche à pain (literally, to be as flat as a bread board)
to be bald	ne pas avoir un poil sur le caillou
to be going bald	perdre ses plumes se déplumer
a wig	une moumoute
to be hard of hearing	être dur,e de la feuille

deaf	sourdingue
to <u>have cauliflower ears</u>	avoir les oreilles en feuille de chou
to be cross-eyed	avoir un oeil qui dit merde à l'autre**
myopic	bigleux, bigleuse
dirty	cracra, crado, cradingue, cradoc (all derived from "crasse" = filth)
to have dirty fingernails	avoir les ongles en deuil (literally, to have one's nails in mourning)

IT'S TIME TO PRACTISE YOUR EXPERTISE

1 Les zizis de vieille bonne femme, ça pue le fauve.

2 Les français ont des pifs énormes.

3 Un beau gosse ne sortirait jamais avec un boudin comme elle.

4 Hé, merde, ça schlingue ici. Y'a un salaud qui a pété! C'est dégueulasse, je vais dégobiller.

5 Ce mec a une gueule qui ne me revient pas.

6 Une gonzesse bien foutue a de longues guiboles, de beaux nichons, un petit cul mignon et un chat parfumé.

7 T'as vu cette espèce d'avorton culotté qui se branle chaque fois qu'il voit la belle Marie?

8 Son paternel a la crève, on dirait qu'il va claquer.

9 Je suis crevé, je vais juste pousser un roupillon.

10 Tes tifs sont drôlement cracra.

1 Old ladies' cunts stink.

2 The French have huge conks.

3 A handsome young thing would never go out with a dog like her.

36

4   Hey, shit, it stinks here! Some bastard's farted! It's disgusting, I'm going to puke.

5   That fellow's got a mug that I really don't like.

6   A well-built chick has long legs, pretty tits, a cute little ass and a sweet-smelling pussy.

7   Have you seen that cheeky little runt who jerks himself off whenever he sees lovely Marie?

8   His old man is ill, it looks as if he'll snuff it.

9   I'm dead-tired, I'll just have a snooze.

10 Your hair is really dirty.

IV THE WEIGHTY MATTERS OF LOVE AND SEX (National Obsession Number One)

The Protagonists

WOMEN

a girl, a bird, a chick	une nana
	une nénette
	une gonzesse**
	une souris*
his girlfriend	sa pépée*
	sa petite amie
his loved one (ironical)	sa dulcinée
his woman, his broad	sa julie*
	sa poule**
his old lady (wife)	sa bergère*
	sa bobonne
an innocent, naive young thing	une oie blanche
a virgin	une pucelle
a spinster	une vieille fille
a coy hypocrite	une sainte nitouche
a shrew	une mégère
a bitch	une garce*
	une salope**
a stuck-up female	une pimbêche

a cock-teaser	une allumeuse* (from "allumer" = to inflame, to set on fire)
a seductress	une vamp
sexy	sexy
an easy lay	un paillasson* (literally, a door-mat)
to be an easy lay	avoir les cuisses légères* (literally, to have light thighs)
a man-eater	une mangeuse d'hommes
a kept woman	une femme soutenue
a scrubber, a slut	une pouffiasse** une roulure**
a whore	une pute* une putain* une morue**
a lady of the night	une fille de joie
a prostitute who solicits from cars	une amazone*
to solicit	racoler
to walk the streets	faire le trottoir faire le tapin* faire de la retape*
a whorehouse	un bordel une maison close une maison de passe un claque*
the madam	la maquerelle*
a dike	une gouine**

MEN

a fellow, a bloke, a chap	un type
	un gars
	un mec*
her boyfriend	son petit ami
	son jules*
a suitor	un soupirant
a virgin	un puceau
a confirmed bachelor	un vieux garçon
a stay-at-home	un pantouflard (from "la pantoufle" = the slipper)
a male chauvinist pig	un phallocrate (from "le phallus")
	un phallo
a smooth talker	un baratineur
a womaniser	un coureur
	un cavaleur
one who likes to go on the prowl for a pick-up (but not involving prostitution)	un dragueur
a casanova	un tombeur*
to be a sex maniac	avoir le sang chaud (literally, to be hot-blooded)
a sex maniac	un chaud-lapin* (literally, a hot rabbit)
	un tringlomane** (from "tringler**" = to have it off)
an exhibitionist, a lecher	un satyre
to suffer from middle-aged randiness	avoir le démon de midi*

to be a groper	avoir la main baladeuse (literally, to have a wandering hand)
a cuckold	un cocu*
a gigolo	un gigolo
a <u>pimp</u>	un maquereau* un hareng* (notice the fishy terminology around prostitution, "le maquereau" being literally a mackerel, "le hareng" a herring and in the female section, "la maquerelle" a female mackerel, "la morue" a cod) un souteneur
a <u>fag</u>, a <u>queer</u>	un pédé*, une pédale* (from "le pédéraste") une tante*, une tantouse* (literally, an auntie) une tapette* une lope* une grande folle*, une folle*
a transvestite	un travelot*, un trav*

GENERAL DESCRIPTIVE TERMINOLOGY

sexy	sexy
sex-appeal	le sex-appeal
to be trendy	être dans le vent (literally, to be in the wind, that is, to fly with the wind)
a young trendy	un minet, une minette
to be striking and elegant	avoir du chien avoir de la gueule
to be popular with the opposite sex	avoir du succès auprès du sexe opposé
to be "with it"	être branché (i.e. switched on)

42

easy-going	relaxe
a stay-at-home	un pot-au-feu ("le pot-au-feu" is a boiled beef and vegetable dish)
a show-off	un m'as-tu-vu
full of oneself	puant,e (remember "puer" = to stink)
snobby, toffy-nosed	snob bêcheur, bêcheuse
fickle	volage
a reveller, a fast liver	un noceur, une noceuse
base, vile	immonde
corrupt	pourri,e (pourri = rotten)
twisted	tordu,e
dirty-minded	cochon, cochonne grossier, grossière
depraved	vicelard,e
obsessed	obsédé,e
repressed	refoulé,e frustré,e
masochistic	maso
to be obsessed with sex	être porté,e sur la chose
to be a cradle-snatcher	les prendre au berceau
to be AC-DC	marcher à la voile et à la vapeur (literally, to function by sail and steam)

The Chase

to <u>go on the prowl</u>, to <u>pick up</u>	draguer
to <u>look for some crumpet</u>	chercher un peu de fesse*
to <u>give someone the eye</u>	faire de l'oeil à quelqu'un
to <u>make sheep eyes at someone</u>	faire les yeux doux à quelqu'un
to <u>devour someone with one's eyes</u>	manger quelqu'un des yeux
to <u>ogle</u>	lorgner zieuter (from "les yeux" pronounced "les zieu")
to cast lustful looks on	reluquer*
to hang around, to come sniffing around	rôder autour
to <u>chat up</u>, to sweet-talk	baratiner faire du baratin à faire du plat à faire du gringue à
smooth talk, sweet talk	le baratin
to be taken in by someone's smooth talking	se laisser prendre au baratin de quelqu'un
to catch someone's fancy	taper dans l'oeil de quelqu'un
to make a hit	faire une touche
to flirt	flirter
flirting	le flirt
love at first sight	le coup-de-foudre (literally, the bolt of lightning)

44

the rendezvous	le rencard
to <u>play footsy with</u>	faire du pied à faire du genou à
to flatter and fondle	faire des mamours à
to <u>feel up</u>	faire des papouilles à
to <u>pet</u>	peloter*
<u>petting</u>	le pelotage*
to <u>paw</u>	tripoter*
to <u>leap on</u>	sauter sur
to <u>neck</u>	se bécoter
a kiss	une bise un bisou un bécot
come and see my etchings	venez voir mes estampes japonaises
my darling	mon chéri, ma chérie mon chou mon petit chou mon cocot, ma cocotte
my darling (woman only)	ma biche (literally, my doe)

Emotions and Conquest

to hit it off	avoir les atomes crochus (literally, to have hooked atoms)
to <u>have a crush on</u>	avoir le béguin pour
to <u>have a soft spot for</u>	avoir un faible pour
to be besotted by	s'enamouracher de

to be smitten by someone	être mordu,e de quelqu'un avoir quelqu'un dans la peau (literally to have someone under one's skin)
to be mad about	être fou, folle de aimer à la folie
to live on love alone	vivre d'amour et d'eau fraîche
to find the man/woman in a million	trouver la perle (literally, to find the pearl) trouver l'oiseau rare (literally, to find the rare bird)
to get one's clutches into	mettre le grapin sur*
to strip	se foutre à poil**
to have it off with, to make love with	s'envoyer* se farcir* se payer* se taper*
to screw, to lay a woman	culbuter une femme* tomber une femme* sauter une femme*
to fuck	baiser** (beware! "le baiser" = the kiss, "embrasser" = to kiss. So never say "je l'ai baisée" when you only mean "I kissed her" because what you are then saying is "I fucked her", a completely different kettle of fish.) tringler**
the bedroom	le baisodrome** (derived from the above)
to get laid	se faire sauter*
to dip one's wick	tremper son biscuit*
a one-night stand	un amour de rencontre

a French letter	une capote anglaise (Just let that sink in. It gives you food for thought about the historical antagonism, remembering also that "to take French leave" is "filer à l'anglaise".)
feats	les exploits (m.)
to make love in a slow, conventional, unexciting way	faire l'amour à la papa
to deflower	dépuceler passer à la casserole** (also means "to rape")
to come	jouir** prendre son pied**
climax	l'extase (f.)
to give a blow-job	faire le pompier** faire une pipe**
69	le soixante-neuf**
to bugger	enculer** emmancher** enfoirer**
to make love doggy-style	baiser en levrette** (literally, to fuck like a greyhound bitch)
a sleepless night	une nuit blanche

Parties

to get all dolled/dressed up	se nipper se saper
a party (with dancing)	une surprise-party une surboum une boum

to whoop it up	faire la bringue
	faire la bombe
	faira la noce
	faire la foire
	faire la bamboula
	faire la nouba
to carouse	faire ribote
to get an eyeful	se rincer l'oeil
dirty jokes	les histories paillardes
	les histoires salées
obscenities	les ordures (f.)
	les saletés (f.)
	les horreurs (f.)
a wife-swapping party with two couples	une partie carrée*
an orgy	une partouse*
to participate in an orgy	partouser*
one who likes orgies	un partouzard*
a sexual orgy involving young girls below the age of consent	un ballet rose
a sexual orgy involving young boys below the age of consent	un ballet bleu
to play gooseberry	tenir la chandelle
dirty flicks	les films porno
porno press	la presse du cul**
a dirty newspaper	un journal de fesse*
drugs	la came
a junkie	un camé
a drug addict	un toxico
marijuana	le marie-jeanne

LSD	l'acid
an LSD trip	un trip
a narcotic drug	un stup (short for "le stupéfi-ant" = the narcotic drug)
heroin	la chnouffe*, la schnouff*
to have a fix	se fixer* se schnouffer* se shooter*

Disasters

to be hanging around waiting, to be <u>kicking one's heels</u>	faire le poireau (le poireau = the leek) poireauter
to stand someone up	poser un lapin à quelqu'un
gossip	les ragots (m.)
to gossip	jacter
to <u>lead on</u>	faire marcher
to break hearts	faire des ravages (le ravage = devastation)
to <u>drop</u>, to <u>jilt</u>	plaquer laisser tomber laisser choir
to <u>be down in the dumps</u>, to feel low and depressed	avoir le cafard
melodrama	le mélo
to <u>take someone for a ride</u>	avoir quelqu'un (used most often by the victim in the "passé composé", as in "il m'a eue" = he took me for a ride)

to be had	se faire avoir
to come home without having scored	revenir la bitte sous le bras** (remember "la bitte" = the cock?)
to steal someone's girlfriend	souffler la petite amie de quelqu'un barboter la petite amie de quelqu'un piquer la petite amie de quelqu'un pincer la petite amie de quelqu'un faucher la petite amie de quelqu'un
to be unfaithful	faire des infidélités
to cuckold	cocufier* (note that "une veine de cocu" = the luck of the devil. It shows that, for the French, being unlucky in love gives you a good chance in other endeavours, so all is not lost and maybe face is saved.)
to put a bun in the oven, to impregnate	encloquer** mettre en cloque** (la cloque = the blister)
to have a bun in the oven, to be pregnant	avoir le ballon*
a backstreet abortionist	une faiseuse d'ange**
to get hitched	se mettre la corde au cou
the mother-in-law	la belle-doche*
a flock of kids	une ribambelle de gosses
the clap	la vérole la chtouille** la chaude-pisse** (literally, hot-piss) la chaude-lance**

NOW GET ON WITH IT

1   Les anglais sont tous des pédés; les français sont des chaud-lapins; les italiens sont des baratineurs.

2   Au fond, les mecs sont tous phallos.

3   Ta copine est une vraie pouffiasse, elle se fait sauter par tout le monde.

4   Fais gaffe au père Dupont: il a le démon de midi, il court après toutes les nanas du bureau, a la main baladeuse et te sautera dessus si tu te trouves seule avec lui.

5   Il est dingue de se mettre la corde au cou: il va se farcir une salope de belle-doche. M'enfin, peut-être qu'il a foutu sa dulcinée en cloque.

6   Y'a que les minables, les refoulés, les pourris et les pauvres cons qui partousent ou se shootent.

7   Quelle bêcheuse, ta frangine, avec tous ses petits minets!

8   Il a le cafard parce que sa nana l'a plaqué après deux ans.

9   Dis, t'as fais une touche avec le type là-bas, il n'arrête pas de te zieuter.

I shouldn't have to give you the translation if you've been studying your vocabulary with diligence. But, anyway, I'll be generous.

1   Englishmen are all fags; Frenchmen are sex maniacs; Italians are smooth talkers.

2   Basically men are all chauvinist pigs.

3   Your friend is a real scrubber, she gets laid by everyone.

4   Watch old man Dupont: he's suffering from the middle-age lust syndrome, he chases all the girls in the office, he's a groper and he'll jump on you if you're alone with him.

5   He's crazy to get hitched: he's going to be landed with a bitch of a mother-in-law. Well, maybe he's got his loved one "in trouble"

6   Only the pathetic, the repressed, the rotten and the poor jerks go to orgies or shoot drugs.

7   What a snob your sister is with her little trendies!

8 He's depressed because his girlfriend dumped him after two years.

9 Hey, you've made a hit with that guy over there, he keeps on ogling you.

V THE NO LESS WEIGHTY MATTERS OF FOOD AND DRINK
(National Obsession Number Two)

Food

food, grub	la bouffe* la boustif* la boustifaille* la graille*
to eat	bouffer* grailler*
to be hungry	avoir la fringale* avoir un creux
to be dying of hunger	crever de faim
it gives one an appetite	ça creuse
shall we start?	alors, on attaque?
a snack	un casse-croûte ("la croûte" here is the end of the long French bread "la baguette"; you would be breaking off a piece of the "baguette" to have a snack with cheese, chocolate, pâté, etc.)
to have a bite	casser la croûte
to have a hearty appetite	avoir un bon coup de fourchette (literally, to have a good way with the fork)
to stuff one's face	s'empiffrer* s'en mettre plein la lampe se taper la cloche

54

to shovel it in	bouffer à la pelle*
to polish off	se farcir* se payer*
a gourmet	une fine-gueule
a glutton	un goinfre
a huge, slap-up meal	un gueuleton*
to be full	caler
to have enough to feed an army	en avoir assez pour un régiment
watery soup	la lavasse* (literally, dishwater)
potatoes	les patates (f.)
beans	les fayots (m.)
cheese	le frometon le frome
meat	la bidoche
tough meat	la barbaque* la carne*
it's as tough as old boots	c'est de la semelle (la semelle = the sole of a shoe)
to hack away at the roast	charcuter le rôti
salami	le sauciflard
the leftovers	les rogatons
pigswill	la ragougnasse*
a fridge	un frigo
to do the cooking	faire la tambouille* faire la popote
awful cooking	la tambouille*

to burn	cramer*
smells of burnt fat	les odeurs (f.) de graillon*
a café	un bistro(t)
a restaurant	un resto
a seedy-looking little eating place	un boui-boui*
a cook	un cuistot*
the bill, the <u>damage</u>	la douleureuse (literally, the painful one)
to <u>fleece the customer</u>	écorcher le client (écorcher = to skin)
this place charges extortionate prices	c'est le coup de fusil ici

Drink

wine	le pinard
red wine	le rouquin (rouquin,e = red-haired)
ordinary red wine	le gros rouge qui tache et qui pousse au crime (literally, the thick red wine that stains and incites to crime) le gros rouge (short for the above)
cheap wine, <u>plonk</u>	la piquette*
a little glass of wine	un petit canon
a litre bottle	un litron
the empties	les cadavres (m.)

56

weak, low-quality alcohol	la bibine*
rot-gut	le tord-boyaux*
any weak beverage (coffee, etc.)	du pipi* d'âne (literally, donkey's piss) du pipi* de chat (literally, cat's piss)
a drop	une larme (literally, a tear)
galore	à gogo (as in "il y avait du whisky à gogo" = there was whisky galore)
a cocktail	un apéro (short for "un apéritif")
to have a drink	boire un coup prendre un pot
to celebrate an event with a drink	arroser un évènement
this calls for a celebration!	ça s'arrose!
cheers!	tchin tchin!
to be partial to red wine	marcher au rouge carburer au rouge
to dilute one's wine with water	baptiser son vin
to be tipsy	avoir un coup dans l'aile être pompette
to have had one too many	avoir un verre dans le nez
to get pissed	se saouler la gueule** se cuiter* se payer une bonne cuite*
plastered, drunk	paf* rond,e rond,e comme une bille bourré,e*

	blindé,e*
	schlass*
to be a boozer	picoler*
a soak	une éponge* (literally, a sponge)
a boozer	un picoleur*
	un soiffard*
	un boit-sans-soif*
a drunkard	un soulard*
	un soulot*
	un poivrot*
to have a hangover	avoir la gueule de bois* (literally, to have a wooden mouth)
to sleep one's drink off	cuver son vin

VOUS ÊTES UN CLODO ET UN POIVROT!

HOW ABOUT THESE SENTENCES?

1 Qu'est-ce qu'on bouffe? Je crève de faim!
2 Les journalistes, ça picole drôlement.

3 Les anglais sont bien sympas mais leur tambouille est dégueulasse.

4 Venez prendre un pot dimanche.

5 Oh merde, j'ai cramé la bidoche.

6 Les goinfres se sont farcis tout le rôti.

7 On a fait la nouba chez les Dupont: y'avait du champagne à gogo, tout le monde était paf, ça dégueulait partout.

1 What are we eating? I'm dying of hunger!

2 Journalists are real boozers.

3 The English are awfully nice but their cooking is disgusting.

4 Come and have a drink on Sunday.

5 Oh hell, I burnt the meat.

6 The gluttons polished off all the roast.

7 We whooped it up at the Duponts: there was champagne galore, everyone was drunk, people were puking everywhere.

VI AGGRO

With your average Frog bristling with impatience towards all other mortals, it is inevitable that there should be a number of words describing forms of aggression or the threat and result of its use.

chicken	dégonflé,e
to chicken out	se dégonfler (literally, to lose all one's air)
cowardly, lily-livered	froussard,e trouillard,e
fear	la frousse la pétoche la trouille
to be afraid	avoir la frousse avoir la pétoche avoir la trouille avoir les jetons (pronounce this "chton")
to squabble	se chamailler
to get cross	se foutre** en rogne se foutre** en boule
to be hopping mad	être furax* être furibard,e* être furibond,e*
to tell someone off	attraper quelqu'un passer un savon à quelqu'un secouer les puces à quelqu'un (literally, to shake someone's fleas)

	enguirlander*
	engueuler**
to get a telling off	se faire attraper
	se faire passer un savon
	se faire secouer les puces
	se faire enguirlander*
	se faire engueuler**
	se faire sonner les cloches
a row	une prise de bec*
a rumpus	un chahut
to rag the schoolmaster	chahuter le prof
a fight between women	un crêpage de chignon (le chignon = bun, the hairstyle; crêper = to tease, to crimp hair, so you get the image of women tearing at each other's hair in that nasty female way of fighting)
to kick up a stink, to make a racket	faire du boucan
	faire du raffut
	faire du barouf
to yell	gueuler**
there is going to be trouble	ça va barder
	ça va chauffer
	il va y avoir du grabuge
	il va y avoir de la casse (violent trouble)
things are heating up	ça barde
	ça sent le roussi (roussi = burnt, scorched)
to give someone a rough time	faire passer un mauvais quart d'heure à quelqu'un
to be on the verge of doing something nasty	aller faire un malheur (as in "je vais faire un malheur" = I'm

	about to do something horri-ble)
to be at one another's throats	se bouffer le nez*
to slap	allonger une baffe
	flanquer une baffe
	ficher* une baffe
	foutre** une baffe
a <u>clout</u>	une beigne
	une taloche
	un marron
	une châtaigne
	une pêche
a black eye	un oeil au beurre noir
a knock, a blow	un gnon
to scuffle, to brawl	se bagarrer
a scuffle, a brawl	une bagarre
a spanking	une fessée
to <u>fly at</u>	voler dans les plumes de*
to <u>have a punch-up</u>	se tabasser
	se taper dessus
to punch someone in the face	envoyer le poing à la figure de quelqu'un
to <u>smash someone's face in</u>	casser la figure à quelqu'un*
	casser la gueule à quelqu'un**
	abîmer le portrait de quelqu'un*
	faire une grosse tête à quel-qu'un
to <u>give someone a hiding/ thrashing</u>	flanquer une trempe/raclée à quelqu'un
	ficher* une trempe/raclée à quelqu'un
	foutre** une trempe/raclée à quelqu'un

to <u>kick up the arse</u>	botter les fesses*
to <u>tear one another's guts out</u>	s'étriper*
to <u>send someone flying</u>	envoyer quelqu'un valser (literally, to send someone waltzing)
to wreck	amocher bousiller
to faint	tomber dans les pommes
to be unconscious	être dans le cirage (le cirage = the boot polish)
to <u>do in</u>, to kill	zigouiller

to eliminate (to get rid of or to kill)	liquider
to bump off	buter descendre
to shoot someone	flinguer quelqu'un foutre** une balle dans la peau* de quelqu'un
a gun	un flingue, un flingot
a police van	un panier à salade
prison	la taule, la tôle

QUIZ TIME

1 Les gosses ont besoin qu'on leur foute des baffes de temps en temps.

2 Espèce de salaud, je vais te casser la gueule.

3 Le mec avait tellement la frousse qu'il est tombé dans les pommes.

4 Les gangsters ont été foutus en taule après avoir descendu leurs rivaux.

5 Je vais me faire secouer les puces parce que j'ai foutu un oeil au beurre noir à mon frangin.

1 Kids need to be slapped from time to time.

2 You bastard, I'll smash your face in.

3 The guy was so scared he fainted.

4 The gangsters were thrown into prison after having bumped off their rivals.

5 I'm going to get a telling off because I gave my brother a black eye.

VII MONEY MATTERS

money	le fric
	le pognon
	le pèze
	la galette
	la braise
	l'oseille (f.)
	les ronds (m.)
	le flouse
loose change	la ferraille (literally, scrap iron)
francs	les balles (f.) (as in "ça coûte quinze balles" = it costs fifteen francs)
10,000 francs	une brique
to be broke	être fauché,e
	être à sec
to not have a bean	ne pas avoir un radis (le radis = radish)
	ne pas avoir un rond
filthy rich	rupin,e*
a spoiled daddy's boy	un fils à papa
to be loaded	être plein,e aux as
mean	radin,e
a skin-flint	un grippe-sous
to fork out	casquer

to blow	claquer
to be had	se faire avoir
to con, to rip off	rouler
	couillonner**
it's a fake, it's imitation	c'est du toc
junk, rubbish	de la camelote
expensive	chéro
free	à l'oeil
profit	le bénef (short for "le bénéfice" = the gain, profit)

PRACTICE MAKES PERFECT

1 Dis, t'as du fric à me passer? Je suis fauché et je dois 100 balles à mon copain.
2 Ce petit fils à papa a claqué un pognon fou sur de la camelote.
3 J'ai eu ces billets à l'oeil.
4 Ce salaud t'a roulé: t'as casqué une fortune pour du toc.

1 Hey, have you got any money to lend me? I'm broke and I owe my friend 100 francs.
2 That little daddy's boy blew an awful lot of money on junk.
3 I got these tickets free.
4 That bastard ripped you off: you forked out a fortune on imitation rubbish.

VIII WORK AND SOCIAL STATUS

Work and Jobs

work, the job	le boulot
the workplace	la boîte
to work	bosser boulonner
to work hard	bûcher
hard-working	bûcheur,euse
laziness	la cosse la flemme
lazy	flemmard,e
to be bone-idle	avoir un poil dans la main
a failure	un raté, une ratée
to exploit	faire suer le burnous* (suer = to perspire, le burnous = an Arabian robe-like garment; from the good old days of the Empire when one made the Arabs work like slaves)
to sack , to kick out	vider (literally, empty out) foutre** à la porte
to have friends in the right places	avoir du piston
string-pulling	le piston

to pull strings on behalf of someone	pistonner quelqu'un
to <u>grease someone's palm</u>	graisser la patte à quelqu'un*
a bigwig	une grosse légume un gros bonnet une huile
a <u>cop</u>, a policeman	un flic un poulet un keuf
the <u>fuzz</u>, the police	la flicaille*
down with the pigs!	mort aux vaches!**
a cop on two wheels	une vache à roulettes**
a member of the security/espionage services	un barbouze
a bodyguard	un gorille
a <u>quack</u>	un toubib*
a teacher	un prof
a chef	un cuistot*
a funeral parlour employee	un croque-mort* (croquer = to bite into, to munch)
a priest in his cassock	un corbeau* (literally, a crow)
a politician	un politicard*
a lady lavatory attendant	une dame-pipi*
a cobbler	un bouif*
a painter (the artistic sort)	un barbouilleur* (barbouiller = to smear, to scrawl)
third-rate paintings	les croûtes* (f.)
a third-rate book, film or other work of art	un navet

a paper-pusher (usually a bureaucrat)	un rond-de-cuir*
a soldier	un troufion*

QUAND J'SUIS GRAND, J'VAIS ÊTRE TOUBIB ET AVOIR PLEIN DE FRIC!

Social Status and Political Affiliation

a <u>hick</u>, a <u>bumpkin</u>	un plouc, une ploucquesse* un pécore* un péquenaud* un pedzouille*

a peasant	un cul-terreux** (literally, one whose arse is covered in earth) un bouseux** (from "la bouse de vache" = cow dung)
the country (as opposed to the city)	la cambrousse*
the sticks	la brousse*
a village	un patelin*
a real hole	un trou* un bled*
to live in the back of beyond	habiter au feu de dieu habiter à perpète ("perpète" is short for "la perpétuité", conveying the notion of great distance)
a tramp	un clodo*
the lower classes, the masses	le populo*
a prole (proletarian)	un prolo*
an aristocrat	un aristo*
the upper crust	le gratin
a Parisian	un parigot, une parigote* (Parisians hold a high rank in the social hierarchy; provincials are considered virtually subhuman)
a reactionary	un réac*
a fascist	un facho*
a commie	un coco*
an anarchist	un anar*

a <u>demo</u>

une manif (short for "la manifestation" = the demonstration)

TEST YOUR KNOWLEDGE

1 Les seules gonzesses qui sont promues dans cette sale boîte sont les pouffiasses qui se laissent baiser par le patron ou les salopes qui ont du piston.

2 Les toubibs donnent beaucoup de boulot aux croque-morts.

3 Un plouc, ça se voit à dix mètres.

4 La punition la plus sévère pour les aristos, à l'époque des rois, c'était l'exil à la cambrousse.

5 Comment, ma fille épouser un cul-terreux et aller habiter à perpète dans un bled perdu? Pas question.

6 A la manif, les fachos ont foutu une trempe aux cocos.

1 The only women who get promoted in this damn company are the sluts who let the boss screw them or the bitches who have friends in the right places.

2 Quacks give a lot of work to undertakers.

3 You can tell a hick ten metres away.

4 In the days of the kings the most severe punishment for the aristocrats was exile to the country.

5 What, my daughter marry a peasant and live in the back of beyond, in some godforsaken hole? Certainly not.

6 At the demo the fascists gave the commies a thrashing.

IX INDULGING IN RACISM, XENOPHOBIA AND DISRESPECT FOR ONE'S ELDERS

Despite the centuries of animosity between the English and the French, Froggies have been unable to come up with any derogatory term for English or British. The pathetic expressions "les rosbifs" (the roast beefs) or "les biftecks" (the steaks) are hardly likely to set the blood boiling; they are not used a great deal anyway. To be sure, it is better to be known as a beef-eater than as a devourer of slithery, vile frogs. That the French consider the English to be double-dealers, hypocrites and experts in the art of the underhand trick comes through in their use of "la perfide Albion" (perfidious Albion) to designate Britain and of "filer à l'anglaise" for "to take French leave" (ha!), but for the individual Englishman there is no venomous word.

a kraut	un boche**
	un chleuh**
	un fritz**
	un frisé**
	un fridolin**
a dago	un rastaquouère** (this has generally meant a greasy foreigner but usually equals dago)
a wop	un rital**
	un macaroni**
a yank	un amerloque*
	un amerluche*
	un ricain*
a Russian	un ruski*
	un ruskof*
a chink	un chinetoque**

a <u>wog</u>, a <u>nigger</u>	un bougnoule**
	un moricaud**
	un nègre*
an Arab	un bougnoule**
	un bicot**
a North African Arab (the French bugbear)	un raton** (gives rise to "la ratonnade" = mob Arab-bashing)
	un melon**
	un crouille**
	un noraf
a <u>kike</u>	un youpin**
	un youtre**
Jewish	baptisé au sécateur* (literally, baptised with pruning shears)
a <u>prod</u>	un parpaillot*
an <u>old grandad</u>	un vieux pépé*
an <u>old granny</u>	une vieille mémé*
an <u>old biddy</u>	une vieille toupie*
an <u>old fogey</u>	un vieux schnoque*
	un vieux bonze*
an <u>old hag</u>, a <u>crone</u>	une vieille bique* (la bique = the nanny-goat)
	une vieille rombière*
	une vieille taupe*
to speak pidgin French	parler petit nègre
	parler le français comme une vache espagnole

HERE IS ANOTHER EXERCISE FOR YOU

1 Les boches bossent dur, mais les ritals sont flemmards.
2 C'est vrai que les nègres ont de grandes verges?

3 Les amerloques sont de grands enfants.

4 Les medias, c'est rempli de youpins.

5 C'est un quartier de ratons.

6 Allez, bouge ton cul, vieille bique.

7 Moi, j'peux pas sentir les vieux schnoques.

1 Krauts work hard, but wops are lazy.

2 Is it true that niggers have big cocks?

3 Americans are big kids.

4 The media are full of kikes.

5 It's an Arab neighbourhood.

6 Come on, move your arse, old hag.

7 I can't stand old fogeys.

X TO EXIT RAPIDLY

to push off, to get the hell out filer
            se barrer
            se tailler
            se tirer
            déguerpir
            se débiner
            ficher*/foutre** le camp

to hurry up   se magner
            se dégrouiller
            se grouiller

on your way! get out!   allez, oust!
            dégagez!
            débarrassez le plancher!

to kick out   vider
            balancer
            foutre** à la porte

APPLY YOUR KNOWLEDGE

1 Hé, les mômes, foutez-moi le camp d'ici! Allez, magnez-vous ou j'appelle les flics.

2 Filons avant que la maternelle n'arrive.

1 Hey, kids, clear off! Come on, hurry up or I'll call the cops.

2 Let's get the hell out of here before the old lady comes.

XI POSITIVE THINKING

Although the Frenchman's bent is for the scathing remark, he *is* able to whip up enthusiasm.

great, fantastic (used as an adjective or as an exclamation)	formidable, formide
	terrible
	sensas (short for "sensation-nel")
	super
	génial,e
	chouette (when used as an adjective, it is placed before the noun, not after as others are)
	impeccable
	au poil (don't confuse with "à poil" which, as you no doubt remember, means "naked")
	extra
great, fantastic (used only as an adjective)	bath
	chié,e**
	chiadé,e**
	du tonnerre
to have great success	avoir un succès boeuf
to have great effect	avoir un effet boeuf

TRY YOUR HAND AT THESE SENTENCES

1 Chouette, les vacances sont arrivées!

2 Elle est super, ta bagnole!

3 J'ai lu un bouquin sensas.

4 Elle est chouette, ta frangine!
5 Cette pièce a eu un succès boeuf.

1 Great, the holidays are here!
2 Your car is fantastic!
3 I read a fabulous book.
4 Your sister is great!
5 This play had tremendous success.

XII FOREIGN INVASIONS OF THE LANGUAGE

READ THE FOLLOWING

1 C'est un appartement de grand standing, avec parking.

2 Quel était le score au match?

3 Les gangsters ont effectué un raid pendant le meeting. Le hold-up leur a rapporté 10000 dollars.

4 J'ai acheté ce gadget au stand du fond.

5 Au club, certains étaient en smoking, d'autres en jeans et pull.

6 J'ai acheté un sandwich au self-service.

7 Le cameraman a pris des films pendant l'interview.

8 Le leader du parti souffre de stress.

9 On a fait du stop.

Recognise some of the words? "Franglais", that insidious creeping of English words into the French language, is a source of worry to the French authorities but is proving hard to contain. All the words above are used in conversation and in the media; they aren't considered colloquial. Therefore the above sentences are not an attempt at being funny, they are examples of contemporary French! In passing from English to French, however, some words have undergone a little transformation, so here are the translations:

1 It's a luxury flat with parking facilities.

2 What was the score at the match?

3 The gangsters carried out a raid during the meeting. The hold-up netted them 10,000 dollars.

4 I bought this gadget at the stand at the back.

5 At the club some were wearing dinner jackets, others jeans and sweaters.

6 I bought a sandwich at the self-service restaurant.

7 The cameraman filmed during the interview.

8 The party's leader is suffering from stress.

9 We hitchhiked.

From the former North African colonies come some Arab words which are firmly implanted in French colloquial vocabulary:

no; no way; nothing	oualou
a hole (the village-in-the-sticks type, remember?)	un bled*
the same	kif-kif
a little (quantity)	un chouïa
luck	la baraka
not much, nothing much	pas bézef
the boss	le caïd
money	le flouse

IMPROVE YOUR COLLOQUIAL USAGE FROM THE FOLLOWING

1 "Vous prenez du café?" "Un chouïa."

2 Y'a pas bézef à faire dans ce bled.

3 "Tu veux le rouge ou le bleu?" "Oh, n'importe, c'est kif-kif."

4 Le caïd a de la baraka.

1 "Will you have some coffee?" "A little."

2 There's not much to do in this hole.

3 "Do you want the red one or the blue one?" "Oh, it doesn't matter, it's the same."

4 The boss has luck on his side.

XIII YOUR FINAL EXAM

Identify the literary tales or historical figures. Answers, but not translations, are provided on the following page.

1   Ce mec devait être vachement frustré parce que c'était un nabot. Sa bergère, qui était un peu bougnoule sur les bords, voulait toujours qu'il la baise, mais il répondait "Pas ce soir, Josephine" parce qu'il était toujours en train de se bagarrer (avec les boches, les ruskis, etc.). Elle l'a cocufié. Les anglais lui ont foutu une vraie trempe, l'ont exilé dans un bled infâme et l'ont probablement empoisonné avec leur tambouille infecte.

2   Y'a deux familles d'aristos ritals qui sont en rogne et puis le fiston de l'une a le béguin pour la fille de l'autre. Il se la farcit, mais ils ont la frousse de dire à leurs vieux qu'ils sont en-amourachés, alors ils se zigouillent. A la fin, toute la bande de cons chiale et devient copains.

3   Un piaf avait chipé un frome et allait juste le bouffer quand un renard fait un peu de lèche-cul pour lui faire ouvrir la gueule. Le frome tombe, le renard le pique et déguerpit avec.

4   C'était un roi, un gros lard mais pas con. Il est devenu parpaillot pour balancer sa bobonne, dont il avait ras le bol. D'autres bobonnes, quand elles l'emmerdaient, il les a faites zigouiller.

ASSESSMENT

0 correct = Connard!
1 correct = Dégueulasse!
2 correct = Flemmard!
3 correct = Sympa!
4 correct = Sensas!

MERDE ENCORE!

Aux copains chez Angus & Robertson
(le dirlo Barry et sa nana Cindy, Murray,
Helen, Janet, Roz & Jill),
à mon jules et mes mômes

CONTENTS

INTRODUCTION 89

I   *VERBS: The nouvelle conjugaison* 91
The MOI-JE Syndrome 91
"Code" Conjugations 92

II   *SUFFIXES: Instruments of contempt and belittlement*   93

III   *LES BEAUX GESTES: French sign language* 96

IV   *GUILLOTINED FRENCH: From aristo to socialo* 101
(Plus yoof-talk = vive les ados!) 104

V   *COUNTING IN FRENCH: Some numbers are more
equal than others* 105
Un, Deux, Trois 105
The Frogclock 109

VI   *SOUND EFFECTS: Gurgle, splash, hiccup!* 111

VII   *THE MOST POPULAR INGREDIENTS OF
FRENCH IDIOMS: Food and animals* 115
Yum Yum, Dribble Dribble 115
    That yukky French food 120
Animals' Names Taken in Vain 122
    Animalspeak 133

VIII   *ANATOMY OF A FROG: A study of vital organs* 134
The Liver 134
The Nose 135
The Tongue 137
"Le Derrière" 138
Other Organs: A Linguistic Potpourri 139

Frog Pathology 147
   Medicines 147
   Hygiene 147
   Death 148

IX   *APPEE BEURZDÉ TOOH YOOH: Franglais as she
is spoke* 151

X   *ALLONS ENFANTS: Kids and kiddie talk* 155
The Au-pair's Guide to Kiddie Talk 155
"Le Français méprise la jeunesse" 156

XI   *THE COCORICO SYNDROME: Roosters rule ok* .. 158
   A cocorico note: Frogs on wheels 163

XII   *GEOGRAPHY À LA FRANÇAISE: A linguistic study* 166
Professor Franchouillard's Geography Lesson 166
Notes on the Natives 169
   Gallus lutetiae snobinardus 169
   Gallus lutetiae intello-snobinardus 171
   Provincial brethren 172

XIII   *YOUR PH.D. EXAM* 173

INTRODUCTION

Before reading this book, you should have digested or at least nibbled at the contents of its predecessor, *MERDE! The REAL French You Were Never Taught at School*. It's not just that I want you to buy both books ("cela va sans dire") but I shall at times in this book assume knowledge acquired in the first.

To give newcomers to our linguistic venture a hint of the value of our previous study, think of the importance of possessing "merde" in your vocabulary. People who have changed the course of history have used it, so why should you lose out on such great moments as when Napoleon told Talleyrand: "Vous êtes de la merde dans un bas de soie." (You're shit in silk stockings)? Surely you know of the moment of the word's apotheosis when General Cambronne, having been called upon to surrender at the battle of Waterloo, yelled it out to the British forces, thus immortalising the five-letter word known ever after as "le mot de Cambronne".

Now, if you enjoyed *MERDE!* and with it finally broke the code of those French conversations which had always eluded you, restricted as you were to the French you were fed at school, you will have appreciated the fact that language is not just an accumulation of words but also a key to the spirit and to the character of the people who speak it. You will also, I hope, have had a good laugh in the process. What I offer here is further exploration of colloquial vocabulary and idioms and, through them, deeper insights into the French psyche. French idioms are often very funny, based as they are on concrete and colourful imagery. I'll give you a few examples just to arouse your interest.

Picture this: **"enculer les mouches"**, a priceless image! As you may remember from *MERDE!*, that translates as "to bugger

89

flies", an image used to mean "to nit-pick, to split hairs", but how much more colourful than the English translation! So there will be elements of scatology in this book (hurray!) but you must learn to accept that urino-anal imagery, so frequently used by the French, is not necessarily rude. For example, there are two perfectly ordinary and acceptable names for colours which are in the above-mentioned genre:

1   **"couleur caca d'oie"** means literally "goose-shit coloured", yet is a normal description for a yellowish-green hue and if Zola can use it in his books, why shouldn't it be part of your vocabulary?

2   **"une couleur pisseuse"** (literally, a urine-like colour) means a wishy-washy, insipid colour.

One more splendid expression, while we're on the subject, to illustrate the concrete nature of many French idioms: **"autant pisser dans un violon"** (literally, one may as well piss in a violin) is used to express frustration, lack of progress, banging one's head against a brick wall. Finally, to show that the visual brilliance of French idioms does not depend merely on excretion: **"sucrer les fraises"** (literally, to sugar the strawberries) describes someone, usually an old person, who has the shakes. Can't you just picture the movement of a hand shaking sideways as it would when sprinkling sugar over strawberries?

I

VERBS:
The nouvelle conjugaison

(Well, not nouvelle to the Frogs,
but probably nouvelle to you.)

THE MOI-JE SYNDROME

The French like emphasis in speech. This has meant that single pronouns have been found wanting. Therefore, one finds the use of double pronouns, particularly in the first persons singular and plural where this need to underline, allied to French egocentricity and mania for individualism, has given rise to the **moi-je** syndrome:

Moi, j'aime pas ce mec. (I don't like that fellow.)

Moi, je suis contre. (I'm against it.)

Moi, je vais te foutre mon poing sur la gueule. (I'm going to punch your face in.)

Special attention needs to be paid to the first person plural, which, you have learned, is "nous". So it still is, but it has been subverted by the now ubiquitous "on", which has graduated from being the indefinite third person singular pronoun ("on dit que" = it is said that) to being the second half of the double pronoun, "nous, on". Worse, the agreement of participle or adjective is with the first person plural, even if "nous" is left out and the verb itself is in the third person singular:

Nous, on est dégoûtés. (We're disgusted.)

Avec les copains, on est allés au cinoche. (We went to the flicks with some mates.)

Disgusting, say the grammar purists! (Mr Grammar Purist, ever heard of the ostrich or the dodo?)

So, for a final look, an example for each pronoun:

Moi, je suis belle, intelligente et cultivée. (I'm pretty, intelligent and cultured.)

Toi, t'es un pauvre con. (You're a pathetic idiot.)

Elle, elle est moche comme un pou. (She's very ugly, as ugly as sin; she's a dog.)

Nous, on en a marre. (We're fed up.)

Vous, vous êtes des emmerdeurs. (You're all pains in the neck.)

Eux, ils sont débiles. (They're idiots, they're stupid.)

CODE CONJUGATIONS

To joke about clodhopping peasants or underdeveloped Africans as they often do, to their great amusement, the French have "code" conjugations of which you should be aware, otherwise you'll miss the reference (try reading *Tintin au Congo* without such knowledge!). The joke-peasant says "j'avions", "j'étions", and "je vas" and is prone to answering a question with "'têt ben qu'oui, 'têt ben qu'non" (in other words, "peut-être bien que oui, peut-être bien que non" = maybe I will, maybe I won't; maybe it is, maybe it isn't). Meanwhile, in "petit nègre" (pidgin French), the first person singular is "moi y'en a" plus an infinitive, as in "moi y'en a vouloir" (I want); "moi y'en a pas être" (I'm not). The articles "le" and "la" become "li", and "monsieur" becomes "missié". Hence, one could have "Missié Tintin, moi y'en a pas avoir vu li chien Milou" (I haven't seen your dog Milou, Mr Tintin), or "moi y'en a vouloir toi donner fusil" (I want you to give me the rifle).

II

SUFFIXES:
Instruments of contempt and belittlement

So you think that suffixes are just another boring little grammatical item? Not in French, where some are invested with great power. The French, with their superiority complex, make much use of suffixes to express contempt and belittlement. Here are the basic ones with a few examples of each (and once you have mastered them, you can coin your own words).

For belittling, meet monsieur –(a)illon:

un avocaillon (from "avocat" = lawyer) — a small-town lawyer

un curaillon (from "curé" = priest) — a village priest

un moinillon (from "moine" = monk) — an inconsequential monk

un criticaillon (from "critique" = critic — literary, artistic, etc.) — a two-bit critic

un écrivaillon (from "écrivain" = writer) — a two-bit writer

Meet his many offspring: –(a)iller, –(a)illerie, –(a)illeur:

discutailler (from "discuter" = to discuss) — to quibble

la politicaillerie (from "la politique" = politics) — petty politics

un rimailleur (from "rime" = rhyme) — a poetaster, rhymester

Meet monsieur –**ton**:

un chèqueton (from "chèque" = cheque) — a cheque

un naveton (from "un navet" = a third-rate work of art) — a third-rate work of art

un cureton (from "curé" = parish priest) — a village priest

For contempt, meet monsieur –**ard** and madame –**arde**:

un(e) banlieusard(e) (from "la banlieue" = the suburbs) — a suburbanite

snobinard(e) (from "snob") — snooty

un politicard — a politician

froussard(e) (from "la frousse" = fear) — yellow-bellied, scaredy-cat

un(e) soulard(e) (from "soûl" = drunk)

un(e) soiffard(e) (from "soif" = thirst) — a soak, pisspot, piss-artist

un(e) fêtard(e) (from "la fête" = a good time) — a roisterer

un(e) bondieusard(e) (from "le bon Dieu" = God) — an excessively, narrow-mindedly pious person

For underlining a point, meet monsieur et madame –issime, who can be used to emphasise positive as well as negative qualities, depending on what they are tagged on to:

nullissime (from "nul")	totally useless, worthless
gravissime (from "grave")	extremely serious
rarissime (from "rare")	very rare
richissime (from "riche")	phenomenally rich, loaded

III

LES BEAUX GESTES:
French sign language

Platitude: the French gesticulate when they speak. Revelation: they are not always merely flapping about; some gestures are a language on their own and need translation. Be very attentive and practise in front of your mirror. (All instructions are given for right-handers; left-handers should adapt them accordingly.)

1 Va te faire foutre!
The king of gestures, known as "le bras d'honneur" (literally, gesture of esteem, respect, homage — a supreme irony). Absolutely vital in all situations, especially when driving.
Meaning: Get stuffed! Up yours! Fuck you!
Method: Right arm stretched out, smack your left hand palm down on the right arm, just above the elbow, making the forearm spring sharply upwards.

2 J'en ai ras le bol.

Meaning: I've had it up to here, I'm fed up.

Method: Using your right hand, palm facing downwards, trace a quick imaginary line from left to right, level with your eyebrows or across the top of your head.

3 Quelle barbe! Qu'est-ce qu'il/elle est rasoir!

Meaning: What a bore, what a drag! What a bore he/she is!

Method: Loosely bend the fingers of your right hand, then stroke your right cheek up and down with the back of your fingers, between the first and second joints.

4 Barrons-nous!

Meaning: Let's get the hell out of here!

Method: Both hands flat, palms facing downwards, smack the back of the right hand with the left palm.

5 Y'a quelqu'un qui a un verre dans le nez!

Meaning: Someone's had too much to drink!

Method: Form an "o" with the fingers of your right hand, making a very loose fist. Put it in front of your nose, facing straight ahead, and make a turning, screwing motion, right to left (90 degrees will do).

6 Mon oeil!

Meaning: My eye! My foot!

Method: Pull the skin below your right eye downwards, using only your right index finger.

7 Aïe, aïe, aïe, aïe, aïe!

Meaning: Uh oh, someone is in trouble!

Method: Right hand palm facing your chest, fingers apart, shake it loosely up and down.

8 C'est pas donné!
Meaning: It ain't cheap, it'll cost you.
Method: Right hand palm facing upwards, straighten fingers upwards and rub thumb up and down the top of the other grouped fingers.

9 J'm'en fous!
Meaning: I don't give a damn!
Method: Right hand out, palm facing upwards, make a hitting motion towards your shoulder.

10 Alors, lá!
Meaning:
1 I really don't know.
2 That's really not on.
Method: Raise both hands towards your shoulders, palms outward. Lower lip should protrude and eyebrows rise.

11 Cocu! (An overworked and much favoured insult.)
Meaning: Cuckold!
Method: Stick your two index fingers up on either side of your head, horn-like, and wiggle them up and down (horns being the traditional symbol of the cuckold).

12 Au poil! Super! Fantastique!
Meaning: Great! Cool! and so on.
Method: Make a "thumbs up" sign with your right hand, and stamp it down slightly in front of you.

Note that the gesture of thumbing one's nose at someone also exists in French and is called **"faire le pied de nez à quelqu'un"** or **"faire la nique à quelqu'un"**.

IV

GUILLOTINED FRENCH:
From aristo to socialo
(Plus Yoof-Talk: Vive les Ados!)

Read the following:

> Napo détestait les intellos.
>
> Le sous-off est complètement parano.
>
> C'est l'intox à coup de gégène.
>
> Le PDG adore la BD.
>
> À la manif, y'avait beaucoup d'écolos rachos.

Mysterious? Well, the clues will appear shortly. Someone who has been guillotined is said in French to have been "raccourci(e)", that is, shortened. This is what happens to many French words. The guillotine effect is widespread in conversation and in media vocabulary. It is most often found in words that have, in their original form, an interior "o" (usually in the penultimate or ante-penultimate syllable), that "o" becoming the last letter of the guillotined word. Learn five words a day.

un(e) écolo (écologiste)   an ecologist (à la Greenpeace or the Green Movement)

un(e) collabo (collaborateur, –trice)   a collaborator (the French World War II version)

folklo (folklorique)   quaint, out-of-date, folksy

rétro (rétrograde)   said of someone or something that indulges in nostalgia, is old-fashioned or imitates a style of the past ("**une mode rétro**", "**une politique rétro**")

maso (masochiste)	masochistic
porno (pornographique)	porno
un(e) aristo (aristocrate)	an aristocrat
une diapo (diapositive)	a slide, a transparency (photography)
le croco (crocodile)	crocodile leather, as in "**un sac en croco**" = a crocodile-skin bag
une leçon de géo (géographie)	a geography lesson
un labo (laboratoire)	a lab
un mélo (mélodrame)	a dramatic scene, as in "**faire tout un mélo**" = to act up, to make a big scene
un chrono (chronomètre)	a stopwatch
parano (paranoïaque)	paranoid
un(e) toxico (toxicomane)	a drug addict
mégalo (mégalomane)	megalomaniac (a common French trait)
l'édito (m.) (l'éditorial)	the editorial
la météo (les prévisions météorologiques)	the weather forecast

Many words just have the "o" added to their shortened state:

un(e) intello (intellectuel, –le)	an intellectual
un(e) socialo (socialiste)	a socialist
un(e) facho (fasciste)	a fascist
un(e) coco (communiste)	a commie
un prolo (prolétaire)	a prole
un dico (dictionnaire)	a dictionary
un(e) invalo (invalide)	an invalid

racho (rachitique = literally, suffering from rickets)	skinny, scrawny
le, la proprio (propriétaire)	the landlord, landlady
le frigo (frigidaire)	the fridge

Or else they are left simply in their guillotined condition:

réac (réactionnaire)	reactionary
la fac (faculté)	the university faculty
le bac (baccalauréat)	the "baccalauréat"
la rédac (rédaction)	the essay (a school task)
l'occase (occasion)	the opportunity
la pub (publicité)	advertising, the advertisement
le bénef (bénéfice)	the profit
la manif (manifestation)	the demo
un trav (travelot)	a transvestite, drag-queen
un(e) mac (un maquereau/une maquerelle)	a pimp/a madam
cap (capable)	able ("**T'es cap de le faire?**" = Do you dare do it? Do you think you can do it?)
l'alu(m). (aluminium)	aluminium
un macchab (macchabée)	a stiff (corpse)
le Boul'Mich (Boulevard St Michel)	(that street in the heart of the Latin Quarter)
le sous-off (sous-officier)	the NCO
l'intox (intoxication)	brain-washing
le, la dirlo (directeur, directrice)	the director (the boss)
le gégène (général)	the general (army officer)

la **gégène** (génératrice)	torture by electric shock (do not confuse with the above "*le* gégène")
le **PDG** (Président-Directeur-Général)	the boss of a company
la **BD** (bande dessinée)	the comic strip

A special note on "la BD": this is a new art form to which much time, discussion, cogitation and ink are devoted. It is a thriving industry and there is even an annual BD festival at Angoulême. To you and me, it is just comic strips but, as it exists in France, where things must be given a more serious, dare I say intellectualised, bent, it is a boom industry, whoops, art form. French children hardly seem to read books any more unless they are in BD form and adults have their own, including porno ones, for their delectation.

YOOF-TALK: VIVE LES ADOS!

As everywhere, adolescents in France (les "ados") are constantly devising new code-words to confound and exclude grown-ups. One youth "language" that has gained much ground is "le verlain", i.e. "le langage á l'envers", where words are broken up and the end syllables put at the beginning. This creates such words as "chébran" (verlan for "with it", from "branché"), by more subtle manipulation "keuf" (verlan for "flic") and the established uniqueness of "beur" (verlan for "Arab" but meaning specifically a French-born child of North-African parents).

Translation of introductory sentences:

Napoleon hated intellectuals.
The NCO is absolutely paranoid.
It's brain-washing through a bit of the old electric torture.
The boss adores comic strips.
The demo was full of scrawny ecology-types.

V

COUNTING IN FRENCH:
Some numbers are more equal than others

"Je n'étais qu'un zéro qui, en chiffre, signifie quelque chose quand il y a un nombre devant lui."

Cardinal de Richelieu
(the number before his zero
being Louis XIII).

UN, DEUX, TROIS . . .

Some numbers are more favoured than others in French as they are part of commonly used idioms. Before you are introduced to them, learn these few colloquial words for things often counted.

les berges (f.) ⎫ **les piges** (f.) ⎭	years, as in "**C'est un vieux gaga, il a eu quarante piges hier.**" = He's an old geezer; he was forty yesterday.
les bornes (f.)	kilometres, as in "**J'ai roulé cent bornes.**" = I drove a hundred kilometres.
les balles (f.)	francs, as in "**File-moi quinze balles.**" = Give me fifteen francs.

Nought (zero) is very important as it quantifies, in the usual negative French way, one's esteem for someone or the level of an activity. We'll start on the other side of the nought and move up from there:

c'est un minus	he/she is a dimwit
il est nul	
elle est nulle	he/she is useless, stupid
c'est une nullité	
il/elle est nullissime	he/she is totally useless, stupid
c'est un zéro	he/she is a nothing, a complete nonentity
alors, là, c'est zéro pour la question!	no way, certainly not!
avoir le moral à zéro	to be depressed, to be down in the dumps
s'en foutre du quart comme du tiers	not to give a damn
à un/deux doigt(s) de . . .	on the verge of, as in "à deux doigts de la mort" = at death's door
en moins de deux	very quickly
en deux temps trois mouvements	in two shakes of a lamb's tail
en deux coups de cuiller à pot	
se retrouver/tomber les quatre fers en l'air	to fall flat on one's back (the image is that of the horse on its back with its shoes ["fers"] up in the air)
un de ces quatre (matins)	one of these days
tiré(e) à quatre épingles	dressed to the nines
faire ses quatre volontés	to do as one pleases, without taking others into account
ne pas y aller par quatre chemins	to go straight to the point, not to beat about the bush

se plier en quatre pour quelqu'un	to put oneself out for someone, bend over backwards to help someone
couper les cheveux en quatre	to split hairs, nitpick
dire ses quatre vérités à quelqu'un	to give someone one's opinion of him/her with no holds barred
ne pas casser quatre pattes à un canard	to be not worth writing home about, to be unexciting (literally, not to break the four legs of a duck)
il y avait quatre pelés et un tondu	there was only a handful of people there (literally, there were only four baldies and one short-back-and-sides)
les cinq lettres	euphemism for "merde"
en cinq sec	very fast, in a jiffy
le mouton à cinq pattes	the impossible, the unattainable
vingt-deux, voilà les flics!	watch out, here come the cops!
se mettre sur son trente et un	to wear one's Sunday best
voir trente-six chandelles	to see stars (literally, to see thirty-six candles, after being punched, for example)
je m'en fous comme de l'an quarante	I don't give a damn (literally, I don't care about it any more than I do the year 40)
un soixante-neuf	a "soixante-neuf" (*that* 69, you know!!!)
faire les cent pas	to pace up and down
s'emmerder à cent francs de l'heure	to be bored to tears
attendre cent sept ans	to have to wait a long time

VOIR TRENTE-SIX CHANDELLES = TO SEE STARS

faire les quatre cents coups   to get into lots of trouble, to
lead a dissipated life

je te/vous le donne en mille   you'll never guess

THE FROGCLOCK

In the seventies, a marvellous slogan was coined which summed
up the drudgery and routine of the Parisian worker's life:
"**métro-boulot-dodo**" (remember from *MERDE!* that "boulot"
means work or job, and "dodo" is the childish term for sleep:
"métro" of course symbolises the form of transport used daily
to get to work). By setting out the daily routine we get the
Frogclock:

7h café;	*14h* boulot;
7h15 caca et un brin	(*17–19h* baise);
de toilette;	*19h* métro;
8h métro;	*20h* bouffe et télé;
8h30 boulot;	(*23h* baise);
12h bouffe;	*24h* dodo.

A quick reminder that "caca" = crap (childish term but used by
all), that "bouffe" = grub, food. What's the "brin de toilette"?
Nothing to do with "caca"; it means a quick wash (and, in
France, that *means* quick . . . see chapter VIII). What about this
"baise" (screw) twice a day? The expression "**faire un petit
cinq-à-sept**" refers to adulterous sex enjoyed between the end
of office hours and the return to the conjugal domain, where
marital sex can be had at the later hour. Speaking of fornication,
you should know that "**un baise-en-ville**" is a small piece of
female hand-luggage owing its name to its original purpose: to
contain the necessary items for an illicit quickie in town in the
days when contraception required bulkier items than the odd
pill. Variation for the young male adolescent: subtract the
"baise" and add a 6h30 "branle" (masturbate), replace "boulot"
with "bahut" (school) and add another "branle" before "dodo".
    A few other times should be noted, as they appear in
idioms:

faire passer un mauvais quart d'heure à quelqu'un	to give someone a rough time (literally, to make someone go through a rough quarter of an hour)
les trois quarts du temps	most of the time
un bouillon d'onze heures	a poisoned drink
chercher midi à quatorze heures	to complicate things unnecessarily

Apply your knowledge:

1 Si Lucrèce Borgia en avait marre de quelqu'un, elle ne cherchait pas midi à quatorze heures; elle lui filait un bouillon d'onze heures et en deux temps trois mouvements son compte était fait.

2 Le concert ne cassait pas quatre pattes à un canard; d'ailleurs il n'y avait que quatre pelés et un tondu.

3 Il est tellement nullissime qu'il faut attendre cent sept ans pour qu'il finisse le boulot qu'un autre ferait en cinq sec.

1 If Lucretia Borgia was fed up with someone, she kept things simple; she just slipped him/her a poisoned drink and in no time at all his/her number was up.

2 The concert was nothing to write home about; anyway there was hardly a soul there.

3 He is so totally useless that it takes him forever to finish a job that someone else would do in no time at all.

VI

SOUND EFFECTS:
Gurgle, splash, hiccup!

You don't imagine that the French go "atishoo" or say "wow", do you? The latter is almost a physical impossibility for them, the letter "w" not really being French (there are very few words starting with "w" in French dictionaries and they are mostly taken from English). To approximate the "wow" sound, it has had to be transcribed as "ouaouh" or, left to its own devices, it would have come out as "vov". Anyway, if you want to understand conversation or liven up your own narrative, you'd do well to learn the following vital sounds.

achoum!	atishoo!
glouglou	gurgle, glug glug
badaboum!	crash!
patatras!	
flac!	splash!
plouf!	
ouf!	phew!
pouah!	poo! (What a stink!)
miam miam!	yum yum!
toc-toc-toc!	knock-knock-knock!
aïe! ouille!	ow! ouch!
heu, euh	um
ben	

111

boum!	bang!
pan pan!	bang-bang! (gunshot)
clac!	smack!
hi, hi	boo-hoo
youpi!	hurray, goody!
taratata!	rubbish, fiddlesticks!
oh là là là là!	uh oh, oh dear!
patati patata	blah blah blah
pinpon	siren of a police car, ambulance or fire-engine
hic!	hiccup!
guili guili	(the noise the Frog makes when tickling someone)
bôf!	(a sound to accompany the shrugging of shoulders to show indecision, indifference or ignorance)

There are certain important nouns and adjectives derived from onomatopoeia:

gnangnan (adj.)	wimpish and given to whining (from the whining sound)
olé olé (adj.)	forward in manner and/or speech; used disapprovingly of such conduct in a young woman ("Elle est plutôt olé olé, ta copine." = Your girlfriend is pretty forward.)
un scrogneugneu	an old grouch (from the grumbling, grouchy sounds he supposedly emits)

le crincrin	the squeaky, scraping sound of a badly played instrument, particularly a stringed one
le tralala	the frills, the trimmings
faire du tralala	to make a big fuss (when having people over, for example)
les chichis	fuss, ceremony ("**Arrête de faire des chichis.**" = Stop making such a big deal of it.)
chichiteux, chichiteuse	affected, lacking in simplicity

A special mention must go to the onomatopoeic "**crac!**". Apart from its sound effect (crack!), the French use it as an introduction to a dramatic event in a narrative. It is a tool used to

113

fulfil their need to emphasise and dramatise. Just before relating the climax of the event, pause, then insert a strong "crac!" and continue your description. Study the following examples.

Ils étaient richissimes et, crac! ils ont tout perdu. (They were extremely rich and suddenly they lost everything.)

Ç'avait l'air de bien marcher et puis, crac! on l'a foutu à la porte. (Everything seemed to be going well then, suddenly, he was sacked.)

Il me parlait de choses et d'autres et, crac! il m'a embrassée. (He was talking of one thing and another and suddenly he kissed me.)

A few more sentences to test your general ability:

1   Badaboum! Elle tombe! "Aïe, ouille! Hi, hi!" elle se met à pleurer. Un scrogneugneu qui passe lui gueule: "Vous êtes bien gnangnan, vous!"

2   Toc-toc-toc! "Qui c'est?" "C'est la concierge. Faut arrêter votre horrible crincrin, y'a les voisins qui rouspètent."

3   Miam, miam, des frites!

1   Crash! She falls! "Ow, ouch! Boo-hoo!", she starts crying. An old grouch passing by yells at her: "What a little whiner you are!"

2   Knock-knock-knock! "Who is it?" "It's the 'concierge'. Stop playing that awful instrument, the neighbours are complaining."

3   Yum yum, chips! (UK)/Yummy, french fries! (USA)

VII

THE MOST POPULAR INGREDIENTS OF FRENCH IDIOMS:
Food and animals

YUM YUM, DRIBBLE DRIBBLE

"Dis-moi ce que tu manges, je te dirai ce que tu es."

A. Brillat-Savarin
(famous gastronome, 1755–1826)

Here is an appetiser (translations at the end of this section):

1   Oh, dis, hé, arrête d'en faire tout un fromage.

2   C'est pas de la tarte de serrer la cuiller à la viocque: elle sucre les fraises.

3   Alors, mon petit chou, t'es pas dans ton assiette?

4   Occupe-toi de tes oignons, espèce de gros lard.

5   Alors, comme ça, j'ai fait tout ce boulot pour des prunes? La prochaine fois, t'iras te faire cuire un oeuf.

Take a nation of predominantly peasant origin where food has a near-religious dimension and you are bound to find many idioms based on food imagery . . . and entertaining they are too! That not very noble vegetable, the cabbage, appears in a number of them, so that's where we'll start.

aller planter ses choux	to retire to the countryside
entrer dans le chou de quelqu'un	1 to hit someone 2 to knock into, collide with someone

oreilles en feuille de chou	cauliflower ears
bête comme chou	really stupid
être dans les choux	to be in trouble, to be in an awkward situation
faire chou blanc	to fail completely, to draw a blank
chou, choute	cute
mon chou, ma choute	sweetie ("mon chou" can be used for men or women)
avoir du sang de navet	to be spineless, cowardly (literally, to have the blood of a turnip)
les carottes sont cuites	it's all over, all's lost
ne pas avoir un radis	to be broke
avoir un coeur d'artichaut	to be fickle-hearted, to fall in and out of love easily and frequently, to fall in love with everyone one meets
occupe-toi de tes oignons!	mind your own business!
en rang d'oignon	in a line in height-order
le panier à salade	the police van, the black Maria
une gourde	a clumsy, clottish person
c'est la fin des haricots	it's the last straw
en avoir gros sur la patate	to have a heavy heart about something (une patate = a spud)
une grosse légume	a big wheel, a bigwig
la fraise	the mug (face)
ramener sa fraise	to butt in
sucrer les fraises	to have the shakes
des prunes!	no way!

faire quelque chose pour des prunes	to do something for nothing (i.e. for no reward or without result)
une poire	a sucker, a mug
couper la poire en deux	to meet halfway, to make equal concessions
les bananes	medals, gongs
haut(e) comme trois pommes	tiny (to describe a person)
tomber dans les pommes	to faint
va te faire cuire un oeuf!	go to hell!
quel oeuf!	what a jerk, what a blockhead!
une andouille	a stupid person ("andouille" is a sort of sausage)
un boudin	a dumpy woman ("boudin" = blood sausage)
ne pas les attacher avec des saucisses ("les" = ses chiens)	to be mean, stingy (literally, not to tie them [one's dogs] up with sausages)
mettre du beurre sur les épinards	to become financially more comfortable, as in "ça mettra du beurre sur les épinards" = that'll make life easier
discuter le bout de gras	to chew the fat, to natter
en faire tout un fromage	to make a big deal out of nothing
défendre son bifteck	to stand up for one's interests
être chocolat	to be thwarted, frustrated
casser du sucre sur le dos de quelqu'un	to say things behind someone's back, to badmouth someone
cheveux poivre et sel	grey-flecked dark hair (often for a distinguished-looking hue)

mettre son grain de sel	to interfere, to butt in
salé(e)	1 piquant 2 dirty (of a story, of someone's actions or jokes, etc.)
ça ne manque pas de sel	it's got spice, piquancy (as above)
un riz-pain-sel	a serviceman (especially an officer) in charge of supplies, a quartermaster
tourner au vinaigre	to go sour (a relationship, for example)
la sauce	torrential rain
la purée de pois	peasouper (fog)
un gros plein de soupe	a fatso
s'amener comme un cheveu sur la soupe	to come along at an inopportune moment; to be irrelevant (a comment, for example)
être soupe au lait	to have a short temper, to blow one's fuse easily
gratiné(e)	outrageous, extraordinary (actions, stories)
le gratin	the upper crust
c'est du gâteau ⎫ **c'est de la tarte** ⎬	it's a cinch, it's easy, it's in the bag, it's a piece of cake
c'est pas du gâteau ⎫ **c'est pas de la tarte** ⎬	it's a tough one, it's going to be rough
tarte (adj.)	silly and ridiculous (describing people or objects, not events)
avoir du pain sur la planche	to have a lot of work ahead

se vendre comme des petits pains	to sell like hot cakes
mijoter quelque chose	to cook something up (mischief, a plot, etc.)
c'est du tout cuit	it's a cinch, it's in the bag
c'est du réchauffé	it's a rehash, it's stale (jokes, arguments, ideas, etc.)
un(e) dur(e) à cuire	a tough, hard person
qu'est-ce que c'est que cette cuisine?	what's all this shady business, all this jiggery pokery?
bouffer (du curé, du politicien, de l'Anglais, etc.)	to hate (priests, politicians, the English, etc.)
bouffer à tous les râteliers	to be a sponger, to cash in on all sides ("râteliers" = dentures, so literally, "to eat from all dentures" . . . yuk!)
un pique-assiette	a scrounger, a sponger
ne pas être dans son assiette	to be off-colour, to be out of sorts (literally, not to be in one's plate)
en faire tout un plat	to make a big song and dance over something
se serrer la cuiller	to shake hands (literally, to shake one another's spoon — well, remember that in olden days the hand was the eating utensil)
être à ramasser à la petite cuiller	to be in a pathetic state; to be washed-out, knackered (a person) (literally, to be in such a state that one can be scooped up with a spoon)
ne pas y aller avec le dos de la cuiller	to act without restraint, to use no half-measures

119

il/elle n'a pas inventé le fil à   he/she is not very bright
   couper le beurre

Translations of the introductory sentences:

1   Hey, stop making such a big deal out of it.

2   It's no easy thing to shake hands with the old bag; she's got the shakes.

3   Well, sweetie, are you out of sorts?

4   Mind your own business, fatso.

5   You mean I did all that work for nothing? Next time you can go to hell.

That yukky French food

The French could put you off your food, you know! I'm not just referring to the fact that they eat those frogs' legs (some 200,000,000 frogs are imported for consumption a year), snails (40,000 *tons* eaten a year), calves' brains, and so on, it's the names they sometimes use. If you were given the following menu in a restaurant, you might justifiably feel an urge to go somewhere else. However, what you are about to read are literal translations of perfectly acceptable, indeed highly appreciated, French comestibles.

MENU DU JOUR
Dribbling-spittle Omelette

Piss-in-bed Salad

Choice of Cheese
(Droppings or The Stinker of Lille)

Nun's Farts
(With Arse-scratcher Jam)

Wine: Pissing Hard

OK, OK, an explanation is coming! In French, the above items would be as follows (and no Frenchman would bat an eyelid).

120

Omelette Baveuse
Yes, "baver" means to dribble. The French do not like dry, stiff omelettes, but runny, squishy ones, so the dribbling image refers to the texture of the omelette.

Salade de Pissenlit
You probably know that "pissenlit" is dandelion, but the literal translation cannot be denied. Besides, the Irish call it piss-a-bed. Actually, who wants to eat the stuff anyway? Can you imagine any dandelion leaves not having been pissed on by passing dogs?

Crottin
So, "crottin" can be equine or ovine droppings; it also happens to be the name of a delightful little goat's cheese.

Le Puant de Lille
This cheese is noted for its strong odour of ammonia, but neither its smell nor its name seems to put consumers off.

Les Pets-de-nonne
Fritters to you and me but what a hilarious image! Actually I'm not so sure that hilarious is the right word . . . let's say disgusting, revolting, yukky . . .

Confiture de Gratte-cul
"Gratte-cul" is the fruit of the wild rose, haws. It seems a shame to give it such an awful name.

Pisse-dru
A Beaujolais brand name.

BON APPETIT!

P.S. You could wash down the exquisite dessert with a sweet Sauternes wine whose particular composition comes from "la pourriture noble" (noble rot), the faint mould which appears on the skin of very ripe grapes when they are bursting with sugar. It is an integral part of the Sauternes wine-making process.

P.P.S. I can't resist adding (and this could be retaliatory ammunition for our Froggy friends) that my dear (English) husband has often asked me to prepare a dessert, the very idea of which I have been unable to stomach, not because of its composition but because of its repulsive name . . . spotted dick (ils sont fous, ces Anglais!). I still haven't brought myself to make it. It must be my dirty mind!

ANIMALS' NAMES TAKEN IN VAIN

Animal imagery plays a crucial role in the highly colourful expressions of colloquial French, often for negative associations: ugliness, stupidity, stubbornness or nastiness. The star animals, those with the longest list of appearance in imagery, are inevitably (remembering those peasant origins of the French) domestic or farm animals, so they'll head our list.

avoir un mal de chien à faire quelque chose	to face great difficulties in doing something
se donner un mal de chien pour faire quelque chose	to bend over backwards to do something, to go out of one's way to do something
. . . de chien (e.g. une vie de chien, un temps de chien, un métier de chien)	lousy, rotten, crummy (e.g. a rotten existence, lousy weather, a crummy job)
avoir un caractère de chien	to have a nasty, aggressive character
malade comme un chien	as sick as a dog, very ill
traiter quelqu'un comme un chien	to treat someone like dirt, without consideration
mourir comme un chien	to die alone, without anyone to care for one
vivre comme chien et chat	to live in constant argument
être chien	to be mean, stingy
avoir du chien	to have a certain chic
nom d'un chien!	darn!
faire la rubrique des chiens crevés	to be a journalist confined to reporting lowly, humdrum events (people's dead dogs, petty burglaries)
une vache, une peau de vache, une belle vache, une vraie vache	a hard, nasty person

AVOIR D'AUTRES CHATS À FOUETTER = TO HAVE OTHER FISH TO FRY

être vache avec quelqu'un	to be harsh, nasty to someone
c'est vache!	that's too bad, that's rotten
un coup de vache	a dirty, mean trick
manger de la vache enragée	to go through hard times (literally, to eat rabid cow)
une vache à lait	someone who is constantly milked by others, a mug, a sucker
ça lui va comme un tablier à une vache	it looks awful, ridiculous on him/her (literally, it suits him/her as an apron would a cow)
pleuvoir comme vache qui pisse	to rain cats and dogs (literally, to rain like a cow pissing)
parler le français comme une vache espagnole	to speak pidgin French, to murder the French language
mort aux vaches!	down with the cops!
une vache à roulettes	a cop on wheels, a motorbike cop
un veau	1 a lazy lump of a person 2 a nag (horse) 3 a tank-like car
pleurer comme un veau	to cry one's eyes out
souffler comme un boeuf	to breathe very heavily or with great difficulty
cochon(ne)	dirty (physically or mentally)
eh bien, mon cochon!	well, you devil!
faire un travail de cochon	to make a messy job of something, to make a pig's ear of something
faire un tour de cochon à quelqu'un	to play a dirty, nasty trick on someone

avoir un caractère de cochon	to be a difficult person
hé là, on n'a pas gardé les cochons ensemble!	hey, don't be so familiar! (literally, hey, we didn't keep pigs together)
c'est donner de la confiture à un cochon	it's throwing pearls before swine
être copains comme cochons	to be bosom pals
des cochonneries ("Il ne raconte que descochonneries.")	dirty actions, dirty stories (All he tells are dirty stories)
de la cochonnerie ("C'est de la cochonnerie, ces tableaux!")	rubbish (These paintings are a load of rubbish!)
les moutons	white horses (the foam on the crests of waves)
les moutons de Panurge	people who follow others blindly (Panurge is a Rabelaisian character)
le mouton à cinq pattes	the unattainable, the impossible
revenons à nos moutons	to get back to the subject
jouer à saute-mouton	to play leap-frog
la brebis galeuse	the "black sheep" (literally, the scabby sheep)
la crotte de bique ("Ta bagnole, c'est de la crotte de bique.")	rubbish (literally, goat droppings) (Your car is worthless.)
une vieille bique	an old hag
mon biquet, ma biquette	honey, sweetie-pie, ("biquet" = kid goat)
une cage à lapins une cabane à lapins	a small, cheaply, badly built dwelling; a rabbit-hutch

ne pas valoir un pet de lapin	to be totally worthless (literally, not to be worth a rabbit's fart)
c'est du lapinisme!	they have too many children! (reference, of course, to the reproductive capability of the rabbit)
poser un lapin à quelqu'un	to stand someone up
un chaud lapin	a hot-blooded male, a sex maniac
un nid-de-poule	a pothole
une poule mouillée	a scaredy-cat
avoir la chair de poule	to have goose pimples
une cage à poules	a cheaply, badly build dwelling, a rabbit-hutch
se coucher aves les poules	to go to bed very early
avoir la bouche en cul-de-poule	to have pursed lips (literally, to have a mouth in the shape of a hen's arse)
quand les poules auront des dents	never in a month of Sundays, when pigs fly (literally, when hens have teeth)
une poule	a tart
mon poulet, ma poule	honey, sweetie, etc.
avoir des mollets de coq	to have wiry, skinny legs
sauter du coq à l'âne	to jump from one subject to another
une oie	a silly goose
une oie blanche	an innocent, sweet young thing
les pattes d'oie	crow's-feet
caca d'oie	greenish-yellow (literally, goose-shit)

WHEN PIGS FLY

QUAND LES POULES AURONT DES DENTS

ne pas casser quatre pattes à un canard	not to be worth writing home about (literally, not to break the four legs of a duck)
faire un froid de canard	to be freezing cold (weather and temperature only)
un canard	1 a rag (newspaper) 2 a sugar-cube dunked in coffee or a liqueur and immediately eaten 3 canard (false rumour, hoax)
un pigeon	a sucker, a mug
se faire pigeonner	to be made a sucker, mug of
couleur gorge-de-pigeon	a colour with silky, changing glints as found on the feathers of a pigeon's throat
il n'y a pas un chat	there is not a soul about
il n'y a pas de quoi fouetter un chat	it's not worth making a fuss over (literally, it's not worth whipping a cat over it)
avoir d'autres chats à fouetter	to have more important things to do, to have other fish to fry
le chat, la chatte	the pussy (the female organ)
appeler un chat un chat	to call a spade a spade
écrire comme un chat	to write illegibly and messily
avoir un chat dans la gorge	to have a frog in one's throat
du pipi de chat	an insipid drink, gnat's piss (literally, cat's piss)
donner sa langue au chat	to give up (when faced with a riddle)
un âne	a stupid person
faire/dire des âneries	to do/to say stupid things

AVOIR UN CHAT DANS LA GORGE = TO HAVE A FROG IN ONE'S THROAT

le bonnet d'âne	the dunce's cap
monté comme un âne	to have a well-developed male organ, to be well hung
du pipi d'âne	an insipid drink, gnat's piss
une tête de mule	a stubborn person of limited intelligence
un remède de cheval	a strong medicine which knocks one out, a kill or cure remedy
monter sur ses grands chevaux	to get on one's high horse
un grand cheval	a horse (describing a woman)

avoir une fièvre de cheval	to have a raging fever
être à cheval sur (le règlement, par exemple)	to be a stickler for (rules and regulations, for example)
entrer comme dans une écurie	to enter a room, a house, without saying hello or acknowledging the presence of others
enculer les mouches	to split hairs, to nitpick (literally, to bugger flies)
tuer les mouches à quinze pas	to have bad breath; to have B.O. (literally, to kill flies at fifteen paces)

130

les pattes de mouche	indecipherable, spidery, tiny scrawl
prendre la mouche	to fly off the handle, to get all huffy
quelle mouche te pique?	what's got into you? what the hell's the matter with you?
avoir une araignée au plafond	to have bats in the belfry (literally, to have a spider on the ceiling)
une punaise de sacristie	a dried up, narrow-minded old woman who spends lots of time in church (literally, a sacristy bug)
une puce	a tiny person ("puce" = flea)
ma puce	term of affection for a small child
secouer les puces à quelqu'un	to tick someone off, to give someone a good telling-off
mettre la puce à l'oreille de quelqu'un	to awaken someone's suspicions
le pucier	the bed (i.e., the flea-bed)
laid(e) comme un pou	very ugly, as ugly as sin (literally, as ugly as a louse)
minute, papillon!	hold it! hold your horses!
pas folle, la guêpe!	I'm/he's/she's nobody's fool! There are no flies on me/him/her ("guêpe" = wasp)

The wild is less well represented, its animals being less familiar than the domesticated ones. However, note:

bander comme un cerf	to have an enormous erection (literally, to have an erection the size of a stag's)

ma biche	honey, sweetie ("biche" = doe)
avoir une faim de loup	to be ravenous
avancer à pas de loup	to move stealthily
un drôle de zèbre ⎫ un drôle d'oiseau ⎭	a weird fellow
un ours mal léché	an uncouth fellow
vendre la peau de l'ours	to count your chickens before they're hatched
un chameau	an unpleasant, nasty person
un faisan	a crook, a shark
un vrai panier de crabes	a hornet's nest (figuratively)
un mollusque	an apathetic, gormless individual
une vieille guenon	an ugly old hag ("guenon" = female monkey)
on n'apprend pas à un singe comment faire la grimace	you can't teach an old dog new tricks (literally, you can't teach a monkey how to make faces)
malin comme un singe	very clever
payer en monnaie de singe	to reward with empty promises, with flowery language and nothing more (literally, to pay in monkey-money)
laid(e) comme un singe	as ugly as sin
une girafe	a beanpole
une grenouille de bénitier	a dried-up, bigoted old woman who spends a lot of time in church (literally, a baptismal-font frog)
poisson d'avril!	April fool!

Animalspeak

No need to tell you that French dogs couldn't possibly go "bow-wow" — imagine, it would come out "bov-vov"! If you wish to venture into the animal kingdom or sing "Old MacDonald" in French, you'd better learn some appropriate sounds. En France:

le chien fait **ouah ouah**,
le chat fait **miaou**,
le canard fait **coin-coin**,
la poule fait **cot-cot-cot-cot-cot**,
le coq fait **cocorico**,

le mouton fait **bêêê**,
la vache fait **meuh**,
l'âne fait **hi-han**,
le hibou fait **hou hou**
la grenouille fait **crôâ crôâ**

Remember especially "cocorico", which is of national symbolic importance (see Chapter XI).

How about a few exercises to see how you are faring?

1   "Alors, maintenant, G. Leculgelé va nous présenter la météo." "Oui, eh bien, aujourd'hui, il fera un temps de chien, il pleuvra comme vache qui pisse et demain, il fera un froid de canard."

2   Dis donc, vieille guenon, quelle mouche te pique?

3   Cet âne, je vais lui secouer les puces, il a encore fait un travail de cochon.

4   Je suis malade comme un chien, j'ai une fièvre de cheval et j'ai la chair de poule.

1   "And now, G. Leculgelé will give us the weather forecast." "Yes, well, today it'll be rotten, it'll rain cats and dogs, and tomorrow it'll be freezing."

2   Hey, you ugly old hag, what's got into you?

3   That jerk, I'm going to give him a telling-off, he's done another messy job.

4   I feel terrible, I've got a raging fever and goose pimples.

ANATOMY OF A FROG:
A study of vital organs

No, we're not going to study *that* organ, you dirty-minded beast! While not denying its importance (ah, zose French loveurs!), there are other bits of the anatomy that play an equally vital part in the behaviour, psyche, pathology and, not least, language of the French.

THE LIVER

Most of you probably don't know the location or function of your liver, but the French are ever aware of its presence and concerned for its well-being. It is an essential part of their obsession with the digestive process — after all, if you have stuffed yourself with food, you have to be sure that it all goes down well. Have you ever suffered from a "liver crisis"? The French do all the time: **"avoir une crise de foie"** is pure indigestion to you and me but, to the French is more localised. To avoid the dreaded "crise de foie", much care is taken to aid and abet the digestive process. For example, a walk after a meal "pour la digestion" is deemed essential. Once, a French boy on a sailboat paced up and down after lunch, to the amazement of his British hosts: he explained that this was necessary "pour aider la digestion". More conveniently, post-prandial liqueurs are called **"digestifs"** and an Italian one, Fernet-Branca, finds great favour in France because of claims on its label that its mixture of herbs helps digestion — a clever alliance of medicine and pleasure.

Of course, carry the obsession with one's digestion to extremes and one has to be concerned with the end product; see a doctor in France about any ailment and it is highly likely that he will ask whether you have been **"à la selle"**. This is not a query about your riding ability (as "selle" = saddle, but here used to mean seat) but about your bowel movements. Note the following.

> **Avez-vous été à la selle aujourd'hui?** (Have you had a bowel movement today?)

> **Comment sont vos selles?** (How are your stools? Description of texture and colour required, so be prepared.)

Patients may well leave the doctor's bearing not a prescription for our much-prized pills but for a box of suppositories. The French are not pill-poppers but suppository-shovers. Many a naive American or British patient in France has been found munching these waxy pellets in total ignorance of the destined orifice . . . now you know!

Here is some relevant vocabulary:

ça me donne une indigestion	I can't stand it, I'm fed up with it, I've had enough of it (said of any situation)
se faire de la bile	to worry oneself sick (literally, to produce bile, the secretion of the liver)
bilieux, bilieuse	irritable
le spleen	melancholy, the blues (though a different organ, the spleen ["la rate" in French] was also presumed to have an effect on one's moods — particularly the darker ones — and the use of this English word was popularised by Baudelaire in his *Les Fleurs du mal*.)

THE NOSE

Listen to two famous Frenchmen:

> *Pascal*: Le nez de Cléopâtre: s'il eût été plus long, toute la face de la terre aurait changé. (Cleopatra's nose: had it been longer, the entire face of the world would have changed.)

135

Edmond Rostand's character, Cyrano de Bergerac:
. . . un grand nez est proprement l'indice/ D'un homme affable, bon, courtois, spirituel,/ Libéral, courageux. (. . . a great nose is truly the sign of a genial, good, courteous, witty, generous and brave man.)

Well, there we are, don't underestimate the importance of the nose, especially when, like Frenchmen, you are endowed with a, what shall we say, powerful, imposing one! Apart from its ability to change the course of world history, judge its place in the French view of things by the number of idioms it has . . . nosed its way into:

passer sous le nez de quelqu'un	to miss an opportunity ("**Ça m'est passé sous le nez.**" = I missed the opportunity, it slipped right through my fingers.)
ne pas mettre le nez dehors	not to go outside at all ("**Je n'ai pas mis le nez dehors de la journée.**" = I haven't been out all day.)
avoir le nez fin	to be shrewd
faire quelque chose les doigts dans le nez	to do something with great ease (literally, with one's fingers up one's nose)
mener quelqu'un par le bout du nez	to dominate someone, to do with someone as one pleases
ne pas voir plus loin que le bout du nez	to lack foresight, to be unable to see the long-term aspect of things
pendre au nez de quelqu'un	to be bound to happen to someone ("**Ça lui pend au nez.**" = He's got it coming to him.)
tirer les vers du nez de quelqu'un	to force someone to tell the truth (literally, to pull the worms from someone's nose)

se bouffer le nez	to have a violent quarrel (literally, to bite each other's noses off)
avoir un verre dans le nez	to be tipsy, to have had one too many
fourrer le nez dans les affaires des autres	to stick one's nose into other people's business
se trouver nez à nez avec quelqu'un	to bump into someone
faire quelque chose au nez de quelqu'un	to do something in front of another with impunity and/or cheek
rire au nez de quelqu'un	to laugh in someone's face
avoir la moutarde qui monte au nez	to get hot under the collar, to lose one's temper (literally, to have the mustard rise up one's nose)

THE TONGUE

Dr Johnson said that "a Frenchman must always be talking, whether he knows anything of the matter or not". A Frenchman without a tongue is a contradiction in terms. Not only a tool of conversation, the tongue is, of course, used for tasting food and wine, for kissing (Anglo-Saxons pay tribute to French propensity in this field by calling tongue-sloshing "French kissing"), and for having a good gossip (a favourite French pastime). A few idioms:

une mauvaise langue	a gossipmonger
tirer la langue	to be dying of thirst (therefore, one's tongue is hanging out); by extension, to be in great need (do not confuse with **"tirer la langue à quelqu'un"** = to stick one's tongue out at someone)

avoir la langue bien pendue	to be very talkative, to have the gift of the gab
se mordre la langue	1 to hold oneself back from saying something, to bite one's tongue 2 to regret having said something
ne pas avoir sa langue dans sa poche	never to be at a loss for words (**"ce mec n'a pas sa langue dans sa poche."** = that fellow always has something to say.)
donner sa langue au chat	to give up (in games, riddles etc)

"LE DERRIÈRE"

If you remember from *MERDE!* the importance of the backside ("le cul" = arse) and of the scatological in everyday vocabulary (knowledge of which is fundamental to the understanding of many a French joke), you will not be surprised to find a number of expressions emanating from that part of the French anatomy:

avoir du cul	to be lucky
l'avoir dans le cul	to be unlucky
avoir quelqu'un dans le cul	to despise someone
en avoir plein le cul	to be fed up with someone or something
en rester sur le cul	to be utterly amazed by something
tirer au cul	to skive, to be lazy, to get away with doing as little as possible (gives the noun **"un tire-au-cul"**)
avoir du poil au cul	to be brave, gutsy (literally, to have hair on one's arse)

péter plus haut que son cul	to think too highly of oneself (literally, to fart higher than one's arse)
un lèche-cul	an arse-licker
un cul béni	a devout Catholic
un cul terreux	a peasant
avoir chaud aux fesses ⎫ serrer les fesses ⎭	to be scared ("les fesses" = bottom)
attraper quelqu'un par la peau des fesses	to catch someone by the scruff of the neck

OTHER ORGANS: A LINGUISTIC POTPOURRI

Other bits and pieces of the body figure prominently and commonly in idioms, so away we go:

tomber sur un os	to hit a snag
il y a un os	there's a hitch
en avoir par-dessus la tête	to be fed up with someone or something
se casser la tête (à faire quelque chose)	to exhaust oneself, to rack one's brains (doing something)
avoir une tête à claques	to have an unpleasant, stupid, stubborn mien, such that your average Frenchman feels the urge to slap it ("claques" = slaps)
n'en faire qu'à sa tête	to do only as one pleases, to go one's own sweet way
faire la tête, faire la gueule	to sulk
une tête/une gueule d'enterrement	a long, sad face (literally, a funereal mien)
avoir la tête enflée	to have a swollen, fat head, to be pleased with oneself

avoir une sale tête	to have a nasty, unpleasant look about one
casser la tête (à quelqu'un)	to get on someone's nerves
tenir à un cheveu	to hang by a thread (**"Il n'en tenait qu'à un cheveu."** = It was touch and go.)
avoir un cheveu sur la langue	to lisp
ça te défrise?	any objection? (literally, does it take the curl out of your hair? A cheeky expression.)
une grande gueule	a loudmouth
ne pas desserrer les dents	not to utter a single word, to refuse to talk
se casser les dents	to fail
avoir une dent contre quelqu'un	to bear a grudge against someone
avoir la dent dure	to be hard and critical
avoir la dent	to be hungry
avoir les dents longues	to be very hungry
n'avoir rien à se mettre sous la dent	to have nothing to eat (in the house)
être sur les dents	to be overworked
casser les oreilles à quelqu'un	to deafen someone (**"Tu me casses les oreilles avec ta musique."** = Your music is deafening me.)
ce n'est pas tombé dans l'oreille d'un sourd	it didn't fall on deaf ears
mettre la puce à l'oreille de quelqu'un	to raise someone's suspicions, to start someone thinking
coûter les yeux de la tête	to cost the earth, to cost an arm and a leg

140

s'en battre l'oeil	not to give a damn about something
ne pas avoir froid aux yeux	to be gutsy
tourner de l'oeil	1 to faint 2 to go off ("**Ta crème tourne de l'oeil.**" = Your cream is going off. "**Ta plante tourne de l'oeil.**" = Your plant is looking a bit sad.)
avoir quelqu'un à l'oeil	to keep a close watch on someone
ne pas avoir les yeux dans sa poche	to see and notice everything, to have one's wits about one
faire les gros yeux	to scold
ça saute aux yeux, ça crève les yeux	it's really obvious
se mettre le doigt dans l'oeil (jusqu'au coude)	to be grossly mistaken (literally, to put one's finger in one's eye — up to the elbow).
à l'oeil	free, gratis
taper dans l'oeil de quelqu'un	to take someone's fancy
faire la petite bouche	to turn up one's nose
une fine bouche, une fine gueule	a gourmet
avoir un chat dans la gorge	to have a frog in one's throat
ça m'est/lui est resté dans la gorge	I/he/she found it hard to take, to swallow
jusqu'au cou	completely, seriously ("**être dans la merde jusqu'au cou**" = to be in deep trouble, "**être endetté jusqu'au cou**" = to be deeply in debt)

avoir le bras long	to have influence, to have the right contacts
avoir quelqu'un/quelque chose sur les bras	to be saddled with someone/ something
gros(se) comme le bras	unsubtle (**"une flatterie grosse comme le bras"** = unsubtle, obvious flattery)
les bras m'en tombent!	I'm amazed, I can't believe it! (literally, it makes my arms fall off!)
être dans les bras de Morphée	to be asleep
j'en mettrais ma main au feu	I am absolutely certain of it, I'd stake my life on it (literally, I'd put my hand in the fire)
ne pas y aller de main morte	to go at something exaggeratedly (**"Il n'y va pas de main morte quand il le bat/quand il se sert un verre."** = He knocks the hell out of him when he beats him/he certainly pours himself stiff drinks.)
prendre quelque chose/ quelqu'un en main	to take charge of something/ someone
mettre la main à la pâte	to muck in (literally, to put one's hand to the dough)
faire des pieds et des mains pour faire quelque chose	to move heaven and earth to do something
avoir quelque chose sous la main	to have something within arm's reach, at hand
se mordre les doigts	to be impatient, to be annoyed
s'en mordre les doigts	to regret something, to kick oneself for something (an action, a nasty word, etc.)

être comme les deux doigts de la main	to be very close (of people)
mon petit doigt me l'a dit	a little birdie told me
ne pas remuer le petit doigt	not to lift a finger
être à un doigt/deux doigts de la mort	to be at death's door
pouce!	time! (to call a halt to a game, to pause)
se tourner les pouces	to twiddle one's thumbs
un coup de pouce	a little push, i.e. help (**"il lui faudra un petit coup de pouce pour avoir une promotion"** = He's going to need someone to put in a good word for him if he's to get a promotion.)
avoir les ongles en deuil	to have dirty fingernails ("le deuil" = mourning)
(être quelque chose) **jusqu'au bout des ongles**	(to be something) totally, to one's fingertips (**"Il est socialo jusqu'au bout des ongles."** = He's an out-and-out socialist.)
la Veuve Poignet	masturbation (**"aller voir la Veuve Poignet"** = to masturbate; "la veuve" = the widow, "le poignet" = the wrist)
lever le coude	to be a heavy drinker ("le coude" = the elbow)
se serrer les coudes	to stick together and help one another
jouer des coudes	to elbow one's way
épauler	to give support

donner un coup d'épaule à quelqu'un	to help someone to succeed, to give someone a helpful push
en avoir plein le dos	to be fed up with something/ someone
se mettre quelqu'un à dos	to make an enemy out of someone
avoir bon dos	to be unfairly blamed ("**il a bon dos le train**" = the train makes a good excuse doesn't it?)
il a une poitrine de vélo	he's a 9-stone weakling
joli comme un coeur	lovely, sweet, cute
prendre/avoir quelque chose à coeur	to take a passionate interest in something
tenir à coeur de quelqu'un	to hold great interest for someone ("**Ce projet lui tient à coeur.**" = He really has his heart set on this project.)
loin des yeux, loin du coeur	out of sight, out of mind (notice that emotions feature in the French expression whereas thoughts do in the English)
avoir des haut-le-coeur	to be on the verge of throwing up
avoir quelque chose dans le ventre	to have guts, courage, balls
se mettre à plat ventre devant quelqu'un	to be obsequious towards someone, to crawl, to toady
le bas-ventre	euphemism for the genital area
autant pisser dans un violon	it's a waste of time, there's no point, it's like banging your head against a brick wall

ça lui a pris comme une envie de pisser	he did it out of the blue (literally, he did it as suddenly as a need to pee)
faire des ronds de jambe à quelqu'un	to bow and scrape in front of someone
tenir la jambe à quelqu'un	to buttonhole someone
cela me (te/lui/nous/vous/ leur) fait une belle jambe	a fat lot of good it does me (you/her, him/us/you/ them)
se croire sorti(e) de la cuisse de Jupiter	to think one is God's gift to mankind
être sur les genoux	to be exhausted, to be on one's knees
avoir les chevilles enflées	to be pleased with oneself (literally, to have swollen ankles)
ne pas lui arriver aux chevilles	to be inferior to him/her
faire du genou/du pied	to play kneesy, footsy
prendre son pied	to have an orgasm
bête comme ses pieds	really stupid
(faire quelque chose) comme un pied	(to do something) really badly, clumsily
ça te/vous fera les pieds!	that'll teach you!
se lever du pied gauche	to get out of bed on the wrong side, to start the day off badly
de pied ferme	with determination
partir au pied levé	to leave without adequate preparation ("partir en guerre au pied levé" = to go off to war totally unprepared)

mettre les pieds dans le plat	to put one's foot in it
ne pas savoir sur quel pied danser	1 not to know how to react or what to expect ("**Avec la belle-doche, on ne sait jamais sur quel pied danser.**" = You never know what to expect with mother-in-law.) 2 to be undecided, to be in two minds
je t'emmerde à pied, à cheval et en voiture	you can go to hell for all I care ("**emmerder quelqu'un**" = to give someone a pain in the arse — remember *MERDE!* The list of forms of transport simply shows the totality of the feeling.)
casser les pieds à quelqu'un	to give someone a pain in the neck

FROG PATHOLOGY

Medicines

Examine a Frenchman's medicine cabinet and you will find amazing numbers of medicines, many of which can be bought over the counter. Great faith is placed in the effect of medicine and the subject animates many a conversation. The French have a high rate of "placebo effect": experiments have shown that sufferers of ulcers given placebos were cured at the rate of 55 per cent in the US, 40 per cent in France and only 20 per cent in Britain.

Hygiene

It's *official*: the pong-factor or stink-factor, what many foreigners have complained of, the . . . er . . . lack of hygiene of the French, has been confirmed by research! Yes, scientific studies conducted by the French themselves have revealed that the average Frog uses only 2.25 bars of soap a year. If you hear "savon" in a conversation it most likely has nothing to do with soap but with an unpleasant situation: **"passer un savon à quelqu'un"** = to give someone a real telling off, a real piece of one's mind. Now *that* "savon" gets used frequently, you can be sure!

Worse than the news about soap is the revelation that toothbrushes are purchased at the rate of one for every three persons a year! Fifty per cent of them go to bed without brushing their teeth! They should exchange their ghastly bidets for an investment in showers, toothbrushes, toothpaste and deodorants. A *French* journalist wrote recently that many Frenchmen smell like kangaroos kept in cages. French kings' stink is well chronicled: one of the recordholders was Henri IV whose odour nearly made his fiancée, Marie de Médicis, faint on their first meeting. She had covered her own body heavily with fragrances from her native country but they proved an insufficient barrage.

Are the French ashamed of their smell? Not really. Why, many think it is sexy. Napoleon wrote to Josephine from Egypt, where he had been campaigning, "Ne te lave pas, j'arrive". (Don't wash, I'm coming.) Consider, if you will, how many weeks it would have taken for him to "arrive" back in France . . . if smell was what turned him on, he was in for a good time!

Death

Disintegration of the anatomy: the Frenchman's natural irreverence as well as his penchant for drama provide the impetus for a rich vocabulary to convey the notion of death. A news report will not say simply that so-and-so died or passed away but that he disappeared ("a disparu") or left us ("nous a quittés"), as though the fellow had done it on purpose. Announcement of death often takes the form: "Tartempion n'est plus" (so-and-so is no more). Here, then, to express the final voyage:

Sartre n'est plus (present tense only, to announce the event as it happens), **nous a été enlevé, est mort, est**

décédé, a disparu, nous a quittés, a été rappelé devant Dieu (well, not applicable to M. Sartre), a trépassé, s'est éteint, a été emporté (accompanied by the name of the illness as in "a été emporté par le cancer").

Or, irreverently:

Sartre bouffe les pissenlits par la racine (notice that in English one says "*pushing* up daisies", whereas the French talk of eating), a cassé sa pipe, a crevé, a clamecé, a claqué, y est resté, a passé l'arme à gauche, a avalé son bulletin de naissance (swallowed his birth certificate).

Cheerio, old boy!

IX

APPEE BEURZDÉ TOOH YOOH:
Franglais as she is spoke

The good news (for you English-speakers) is that Franglais is expanding daily. If the Frogs go on like this, you won't have to bust your guts trying to learn their language.

The bad news is that you have to learn their funny pronunciation (viz. the chapter heading — Frogpronunciation for "Happy Birthday to You", which is sung up and down the land) as well as the arbitrary gender they give the purloined words. The following is a basic list of real Franglais.

l'after-shave (m.)

le badge

le barbecue

les baskets (= sneakers, plimsolls)

le beefsteack (sic), le bifteck

le best-seller

le black-out

le blue-jean

les blues

le bluff

le box-office

le break (= a station wagon)

le bridge (= dental bridge/ card game)

le bulldozer

le bungalow

le caddy (= the supermarket trolley)

le cake (= fruitcake)

la call-girl

le car-ferry

le club

le cocktail

la cover-girl

le cover-story

un crack (= a wizard, an ace)

le dancing

le design

le détective

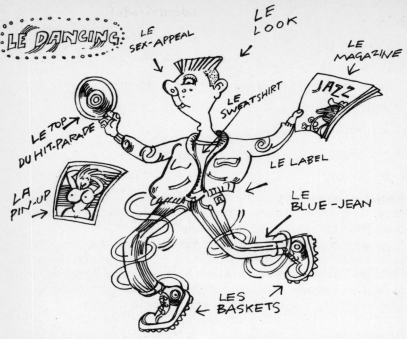

LE DANCING

LE SEX-APPEAL

LE LOOK

LE MAGAZINE

LE SWEATSHIRT

JAZZ

LE TOP DU HIT-PARADE

LE LABEL

LA PIN-UP

LE BLUE-JEAN

LES BASKETS

le discount	**le gentleman**
le doping	**le hall**
l'escalator (m.)	**le handicap**
l'establishment (m.)	**le hit-parade**
le fair-play	**le hold-up**
les fans	**le hooligan**
le fast-food	**l'interview** (f.)
le feedback	**le jerry-can**
le flash	**le jogging**
le fuel (heating oil)	**le joker** (in cards)
le gadget	**le kidnapping**
le gangster	**le kit**
le garden-center	**le knock-out**
le gay	**le label**

le leader

le lifting (the face-lift)

le living (= the living/sitting-room)

le look

le magazine

le manager

le marketing

les mass-media (m.)

le music-hall

le must

le name-dropping

le one-man-show

l'outsider (m.) (in a race)

le pacemaker

le parking

le patchwork

le pickpocket

la pin-up

le planning

le playback

le play-boy

le pressing (= the dry-cleaners)

le puzzle

le racket (the illegal one)

se relaxer

le scoop (journalistic)

la script-girl

select(e) (adj.)

le self-made-man

le self-service

le sex-appeal

sexy

le short (= shorts)

le show business

le sketch (in entertainment)

le slogan

le snack (= snack-bar)

snob

le software

le sponsoring

le spot publicitaire (= the ad)

squattériser, le squat

le standing (= status)

la starlet, la star

le stock

le stop (= thumbing a lift, hitch-hiking)

stopper (to stop)

le stress

le studio (= one-roomed flat)

le supporter

le sweatshirt

le talkie-walkie (*sic*)

le time-sharing

le traveller's cheque

le week-end

These sentences should be no problem:

1   Le cover-story du magazine décrit le best-seller qui va faire partie du name-dropping littéraire aux dîners de Paris.

2   Le look de la saison est un véritable patchwork de styles.

3   Le sketch montrait des pickpockets dans un squat.

P.S. Add to the list most sporting terms, too numerous to be mentioned here (for example, le sprint, le tennis, le crawl, le recordman, le score, le match, and so on).

X

ALLONS ENFANTS:
Kids and kiddie talk

THE AU-PAIR'S GUIDE TO KIDDIE TALK

"Mémé, le toutou, il m'a fait bobo." "Tonton m'a fait panpan parce que j'ai fait pipi dans mon dodo." Got it? If you're going to take care of the little brats, you'd better learn to communicate with them, so the following is required knowledge.

mémé	granny
pépé	grandad
tonton	uncle
tata	aunt
au dodo!	off to bed!
faire dodo	to sleep
le lolo	milk
le nounours	the teddy bear
avoir bobo	to have something that hurts ("**T'as bobo à la papatte?**" = Does your little leg/hand hurt?)
un bobo	a sore
la menotte	the hand
la papatte	the leg/the hand
les quenottes (f.)	the toothy-pegs

le toto	the head louse
le loulou	snot
le zizi	the genital organ (male or female)
pipi (m.)	wee wee, number one
caca (m.) } la grosse commission }	poo, number two
un prout	a fart
faire panpan	to smack
le toutou	the doggy
le joujou	the toy
faire joujou	to play
faire sisite	to sit down

To talk to little children in the idiotic way many adults do, simply repeat part or all of one-syllable words: "fifille", "chienchien", "papatte" ... Note that use of the above vocabulary is not confined to the kiddie community, as you may recall from previous chapters, where mention is made of "caca d'oie" and "métro-boulot-dodo". Many of these words also appear in satirical contexts, so to understand adult jokes, apply yourself to learning kiddie vocabulary.

"LE FRANÇAIS MÉPRISE LA JEUNESSE"
Jean Cocteau,
Picasso, Editions Stock

Do Frogs like children? I am not terribly convinced they do. Before I get pelted with tomatoes by indignant Frogesses, could I simply ask you to draw your own conclusion from the large number of abusive terms used to describe children. Our "brats" is nothing compared with the variety of French names which have the same meaning but are too often used instead of "kids". For a start, even the normal words for "kids" ("**les gosses**", "**les mômes**", "**les gamins**") are often preceded by "sales" (dirty;

used here for beastly, rotten), which does not denote great tenderness. The following all mean "brats", have a note of unpleasant irony, can equally be preceded by "sales" and are quite commonly used.

les lardons (m.)
les mioches (m., f.)
les marmots (m.)
les mouflets, mouflettes
les rejetons (m.)
les moutards (m.)
les morveux (m., f.) (literally, the snotty-nosed)
les chiards (m.) (literally, the crappers)
la marmaille (a group of noisy children)

Their native impatience prevents the French from putting themselves at children's level. They are easily irritated and can be very agile at distributing **"les claques"**, **"les gifles"** (slaps in the face). On the reverse side of the coin, the media often descend to maudlin, glutinous sentimentality, talking of "nos chérubins" or "nos petites têtes blondes" (they cannot be serious!). A final note, and conclude from it what you will, France has the second-worst record after Hungary for accidents in the home involving children.

XI

THE COCORICO SYNDROME:
Roosters rule ok

"Qu'est-ce que la France, je vous le demande? Un coq sur un fumier. Ôtez le fumier, le coq meurt." (What is France, I ask you? A rooster on a dung heap. Take away the dung, and the rooster dies.)

Jean Cocteau,
La Difficulté d'être,
Editions du Rocher

"... forgive me God,
That I do brag thus; this your air of France
Hath blown that vice in me."

Shakespeare (*Henry V*)

It seems a daft idea, though perhaps an appropriate one, to have a rooster — that vain, strutting, loud-mouthed, ridiculous creature — as a national symbol. Napoleon's eagle was certainly a more dignified idea, though he got his feathers plucked just as surely as the neighbourhood barnyard rooster. The Latin word "gallus" provides the symbol, "gallus" being at the same time "the Gaul" and "the rooster". No fools those Romans, they had already remarked upon the Gauls' loquacity as well as their querulous, aggressive natures. Tacitus reckoned that if the Gauls had stopped quarrelling amongst themselves they would have been nearly invincible.

What other manifestations are there of what one could call the "cocorico syndrome"? Before I am accused of slander, allow me to point out that every year books are published in France analysing and usually criticising the French character and how it affects the individual's and the country's life; the French, given to self-analysis ("**le nombrilisme**" = navel contemplation), are quite aware of their defects, and are sometimes even proud of them.

At the national level, the cocorico syndrome is revealed in the need to win acclaim, to have France's "destiny" and importance to the world recognised. It has made some Frenchmen say the most extraordinary things across the ages. Such as:

> "La gloire de la France est un des plus nobles ornements du monde." (France's glory is one of the world's most noble adornments.)

Montaigne

Mr Supercocorico himself, General de Gaulle, was forever proclaiming France synonymous with grandeur and reckoned she existed to "illuminate" the universe . . .

The press still talks of "**l'honneur de la France**" and sees failures or setbacks as humiliations. It is interesting to see how the "cocorico syndrome" has affected the French reading of history. Of course, each country has a selective memory for historical dates. Here are a few which are firmly imprinted on the national psyche, not all of them victorious moments either, though François Ier had a comforting word about that. Faced with defeat at Pavia, he exclaimed: "Tout est perdu fors l'honneur" (All is lost save honour) . . . to each his own priorities.

AD 52 Alésia: Vercingétorix, valiant leader of the Gauls, is beaten by the "sales" (i.e., rotten) Romans, who drag him back to Rome and execute him.

732 (Cocorico!) Charles Martel kicks out the "sales" Saracens at Poitiers.

1214 (Cocorico!) Philippe Auguste socks it to the "sales" league of English, Flemish and Germans at Bouvines.

1431 The "sales" English burn our girl, Jeanne d'Arc.

1515 (Cocorico!) François Ier socks it to the Swiss at Marignan.

1789 (Cocorico!) The French infuse the world with the spirit of liberty, equality and fraternity.

1792 (Cocorico!) The people's army routs the foreign enemy at Valmy.

1870 Defeat at Sedan at the hands of the "sales" Boches.

1898   The "sales" English humiliate us at Fachoda (Sudan).
1940   The "sales" Brits treacherously sink our fleet at Mers-el-Kebir.

At the individual level, we get "le Français frondeur" (anti-authority, ever critical), the opinionated, querulous, restless, contradictory undisciplined worshipper of speech who easily substitutes words for action. Shakespeare and Walpole knew a thing or two about "those confident and over-lusty French" (Shakespeare) and "their insolent and unfounded airs of superiority" (Walpole). Ah, now, speaking of lust, what of that worldwide, self-proclaimed reputation in this field?

The rooster services many hens and makes a lot of noise, but does he satisfy those hens? He obviously thinks so:

> "Le Français est un mâle supérieur . . . comme amant il crée partout." (The Frenchman is a superior male . . . as a lover, he is ever creative.)
>
> Jules Michelet (nationalist historian 1798–1874)

> "Le français . . . c'est la langue même des dieux, la seule dans laquelle un homme puisse laisser entendre à une femme qu'il l'aime." (French . . . is the very language of the gods, the only one in which a man can make a woman understand that he loves her.)
>
> Maurice Bedel (writer 1884–1954)

The Frenchman's ability in what he considers a sport and an art-form resides, as with his intellectual pursuits, more in form than in content. Murmuring sweet poetic nothings that would make anyone swoon with rapture is one of his prize talents . . . yet what good is it to be told that one is a fellow's eternal love when he omits to add "eternal love number 598"? To the Frenchman, adultery is an accepted fact of life and the absence of extra-marital pursuits might cast doubts on one's virility.

Despite the leering, the coveting of the neighbour's wife and the view of sex as proof of sporting prowess and artistic creativity, there are numerous maudlin articles in the press about celebrities' fairytale loves (see *Paris Match*, for example). Nobody actually believes them but everyone still reads the sickly stuff.

The "cocorico syndrome" in its egocentric aspect produces the legendary rudeness and the notorious queue-jumping. A

161

recent European poll is revealing: in a list of seventeen qualities to be ranked in order of importance, the French put manners in only tenth place. (P.S. The British put them in second place, after honesty — another quality that did not fare very well in the French ratings.)

Who says the French don't play much sport? It just depends on one's definition of sport. The expression **"c'est tout un sport"** has nothing to do with athletic pursuits; it refers to the great effort one has to make to accomplish something, as in "C'est tout un sport de lui plaire" (It's very difficult to please him/her).

Recognised national sports are: **"la resquille"** (getting something to which one has no right, getting away without paying for something; for example, fare-evasion), **"la combine"** (scheming, beating the system, working round regulations for one's own benefit) and **"rouler le fisc"** (fiddling one's taxes). It follows from acceptance of these activities that the French are ever **"méfiants"** (distrustful, suspicious) and that one of their reflexes is to search for what might be concealed underneath an action or a proposal. The European values study showed that seventy-one per cent of the French believe that people cannot be trusted. The rules of the aforementioned sports allow for **"la dénonciation"** (denunciation), a favourite French activity, along with its offshoot, calumny. Both make much use of the anonymous letter and reached their heyday under the German occupation in World War II.

The European values study also confirmed the importance of **"l'épargne"** (thrift). Indeed, the **"image d'Épinal"** (= stereotype; from the popular prints depicting typical scenes from French life, which came from Épinal from the eighteenth century onwards) of the French includes the love of a good bargain (**"la bonne affaire"**) and an attachment to gold. There is a fortune of 4500 tons of gold in private hands in France, as much as for the rest of Europe put together.

Speaking of gold, what are the gold medal achievements of our fine-feathered friends, the **"cocoricorecords"** (a term coined by the magazine *Nouvel Observateur*)?

1   The second-highest alcohol intake in the world.

2   The highest rate of cirrhosis of the liver of all industrialised countries (our friend the liver strikes again).

3   The second-highest number of car accidents per head of population, a statistic not unrelated to the first record but by no

means totally explained by it. The "cocorico syndrome" as it emerges in French driving habits deserves a special note.

A cocorico note: Frogs on wheels

Be prepared: the French are selfish, macho drivers who stick close to the back of your car ("**coller aux fesses**"). They flash their headlights and honk their horns in an ever-present urge to overtake and speed away to the next traffic light. The women are as aggressive as the men, and the owners of small cars get orgasmic thrills out of overtaking more powerful Mercedes, BMWs and the like. It might be useful to know some relevant vocabulary and don't forget to perfect your "bras d'honneur" (see Chapter III), as you will need it constantly to express your indignation at nasty French driving, though, of course, as it requires the use of both hands, it might be better to teach it to your passengers so that, unlike the Frogs, you can keep your hands on the wheel.

un chauffard	a reckless, bad driver
faire une queue de poisson	to overtake and cut in close in front of the car you are overtaking (literally, to do a fishtail)
appuyer sur le champignon	to step on it, to put one's foot down on the accelerator (literally, to press down on the mushroom, from the shape of certain old-fashioned pedals)
conduire à la vitesse grand V	to drive at great speed, to go like a bat out of hell
brûler/griller le feu rouge	to go through a red light, to jump the lights
rentrer dans le décor	to drive off the road into a ditch, a tree, etc. (the consequence of the previous activities; "le décor" = the scenery)

se payer un arbre, un piéton	to drive right into a tree, a pedestrian
cette bagnole bouffe de l'essence	this car is a petrol-guzzler
c'est un vrai tape-cul	it's a bone-shaker (literally, it's a real arse-thumper)
un tacot } **un teuf-teuf**	an old, slow-moving car

une bagnole poussive	a slow car
une contredanse	
un PV (un procès-verbal)	a ticket

It is worth knowing that French number plates ("**plaques minéralogiques**") give a clue to the driver's place of residence: the last two numbers correspond to his "département" or, in the case of Paris, to the city itself or its suburbs. The magic number is 75 ("ville de Paris") whose proud bearers can look in condescension on the Parisian suburbanites with their 78 (Yvelines), 91 (Essonne), 92 (Hauts-de-Seine), 93 (Seine-Saint-Denis), 94 (Val-de-Marne) and 95 (Val-d'Oise). All of these can in turn look down with pity or contempt on any other number. On the other hand, driving around the provinces with Parisian number plates can attract "**des remarques désobligeantes**" (unpleasant remarks) about "**ces sales Parigots**" (those Parisian bastards), given that their driving is even more selfish and aggressive than the national average.

Finally, if you want to be like the French, you may scoff at cars sporting the B sticker (Belgium) or the CH one (Switzerland), as the French love railing at these peoples' slow, clumsy driving.

XII

GEOGRAPHY À LA FRANÇAISE:
A linguistic study

PROFESSOR FRANCHOUILLARD'S*
GEOGRAPHY LESSON

Let's listen in to Professor Franchouillard's very own, very typical geography lesson on foreign countries.

Prof. Franchouillard: I shall tell you a joke. There once was a Belgian . . . hee, hee, ha, ha . . . (*He breaks into uncontrollable fits of laughter.*)

We, the audience: Are you all right?

Prof. Franchouillard: Yes, yes, ah mon dieu . . . There was once a Swiss . . (*More uncontrollable laughter.*)

Audience: Please, what can we do for you?

Prof. Franchouillard (regaining his composure):   Listen, the English among you would say "There's this Irishman", the Americans would say "There's this Pole". Eh bien, nous, on dit "Y'a un Belge", "Y'a un Suisse", because the Belgians and the Swiss are so stupid, so thick, so slow! They have such funny accents! They say such funny things as "septante" (seventy) and "nonante" (ninety).

A student: Excuse me, sir, isn't it easier and more logical to say "septante" and "nonante" than "soixante-dix" and "quatre-vingt-dix"?

Prof. Franchouillard: Ta gueule ou je te fous mon pied au cul (shut up or you'll get a boot up your backside). Now, speaking

---

*Franchouillard = colloquial French for Frenchman, i.e., Frenchy.

as we were of those "sales Anglais", we and our language know how to deal with them! No need to remind you of **"filer à l'anglaise"** (to take French leave) and **"la capote anglaise"** (French letter). But do you know what **"avoir ses anglais"** or **"les Anglais débarquent"**(literally, the English have landed) mean? Ha, ha, ha, it means a woman's period has started!!! That'll teach those English bastards to be so arrogant! See in the image the suddenness of the flow of red-coats and the notion of invasion . . . brilliant, n'est-ce pas? As for **"le vice anglais"**, that's homosexuality (or, sometimes, flagellation), and **"anglaiser"** means to sodomise, to bugger . . . after all, we French know that the English are all disgusting poofs, queers, fags. And such hypocrites! In their honour, we have the expression **"le coup de Trafalgar"** which really means an unexpected catastrophe but is popularly used to mean an underhand trick because the English are always playing dirty with their double-dealing, perfidious underhandedness. Anyway, we almost won Trafalgar and Waterloo and we got that bugger Nelson!

A student: Have you any more world views to impart to us?

Prof. Franchouillard: If you have learnt your lessons in our first textbook, *MERDE!*, you will know all about **"les Boches, les Amerloqs, les Ritals, les Rastaquouères, les Ruskis, les Bougnoules, les Bicots"**, and so on. As for our views on others, apart from the Belgians, the Swiss and the English we're not all that bothered, except that, nowadays, we slavishly idolise everything American, all the while maintaining our belief in our own intellectual superiority. But we do have the odd expression that will come in handy:

une querelle d'Allemand	a quarrel started for no good or obvious reason (a throwback to the continuous and petty quarrels of the German princelings of old)
soûl comme un Polonais	blind drunk
avoir l'oeil américain	to have a sharp eye
c'est pas le Pérou	it's not a fortune, it's not a great deal of money, one won't get rich on that

une tête de Turc	a scapegoat, a whipping boy
fort comme un Turc	strong as a horse
le téléphone arabe	the bush telephone
c'est de l'hébreu c'est du chinois }	it's all Greek to me
les chinoiseries (f.)	1 unnecessary, hair-splitting complications 2 red-tape
un casse-tête chinois	a real puzzle, a real headache
un supplice chinois	a cruel and refined torture
boire en Suisse	to drink selfishly, on one's own, in secret
point d'argent, point de Suisse	if there's no money to be had, there'll be no Swiss around
va te/allez vous faire voir chez les Grecs!	go and get stuffed! (cf the ancient Greeks' homosexual leanings)

In contrast to the above, and quite rightly so, you should know that the word "français" appears in favourable expressions (Cocorico!):

en bon français	to put it simply
vous ne comprenez pas le français, non?	can't you understand when one speaks to you? (i.e. why are you so thick?)
impossible n'est pas français	the word "impossible" is not in the French language
une histoire gauloise	a dirty story, a blue story

Everyone knows that there are two basic types of French people: the Parisians and all the rest, "les provinciaux", those poor second-class citizens given to emotional cricks in the neck as they incessantly and enviously stare at the bright centre of all political, economic, cultural, financial and educational life, all the while denouncing "le parisianisme" (the assumption that only Paris is deserving of one's attention). The stereotypical characteristics of the French are exaggerated in the Parisian, who adds to them a heavy dose of arrogance.

Two main forms of snobbery can be found in Paris (overlapping is possible), so let's have a look.

Gallus lutetiae snobinardus (Lutetia = Latin for Paris)
This is the moneyed and/or aristocratic branch.

HABITAT:
"Les beaux quartiers", which are basically the XVIe arrondissement, with some streets of the neighbouring VIIIe, and some streets of the old VIe (Latin Quarter).

MIGRATORY PATTERN:
to the "château" or other "résidence secondaire".

DESIGNATION IN ORDER OF PREFERENCE:
1   A title, however bogus or "du côté gauche" (from the wrong side of the blanket, the term for titles conferred on the numerous illegitimate offspring of kings, princes, cardinals, and so on).

2   "La particule", the prized "de". These two measly letters, which originally meant nothing more than that their bearer came from a certain village, have acquired an aura of grandeur which makes people search desperately for some ancestor who had such a "de", so that it can be tagged on to their own names. Or, if the worst comes to the worst, one can always insert it with impunity or change the spelling of one's name, just as Napoleon III's illegitimate half-brother, who was born Demorny, changed the spelling of his name to "de Morny" and called himself "duc" — so much more dignified.

3   A double-barrelled name — and all the better if the barrels contain a "de", as in Madame de la Connerie de Merde.

4 Choice of first names. Exotic or mediaeval names set one aside from "**la populace**", "**le menu fretin**", "**le populo**", "**les gens communs**", you know, ordinary people.

To demonstrate the above, let us examine the births, engagements and marriages page of the *Figaro*, particularly on a Saturday. Take Saturday, 26 January 1985: on that day, "le carnet du jour" listed twenty-three engagements, fourteen of which contained one or all of the previously mentioned assets. Example:

> Le vicomte Hugues de Monts de Savasse et la vicomtesse, née Chantal de Fournas de la Brosse, M. Yves du Mesnildot et Mme., née Marie de La Bourdonnaye, sont heureux d'annoncer les fiançailles de leurs enfants. . . . [Yuk!]

As for the births section, exotic or mediaeval names given to the newborn were Typhanie, Apollonia, Colombe, Fleur, Solène, Amaury, Aliénor, Héloïse.

SPEECH:
The height of rarefied elegance, becoming thankfully very rare indeed, is attained by those parents who make their children address them by the formal pronoun "vous". It could result in "Maman, vous m'emmerdez!"

The tone of our "snobinardus" friend is not the braying of the English aristocracy but a more refined, slow, measured, assured tone of voice, delivery accompanied by the slight hooding of the eyes and an upward tilt of the nose. Useful long words to express one's amazement at another's vulgarity or stupidity:

d'une vulgarité, d'une bêtise		
	inénarrable	sidérante
	faramineuse	suffoquante
	monumentale	époustouflante
	prodigieuse	hallucinante
	phénoménale	grotesque
	ineffable	aberrante
	inouïe	épouvantable

All give the notion of "extraordinary" and/or "breath-taking".

Gallus lutetiae intello-snobinardus

This creature can belong to the previous crowd but its genus can exercise a tyrannical exclusivism all of its own. Its main weapon is manipulation of the spoken word, the more abstruse, pretentious, incomprehensible and recondite, the better. The "snowing" of others to prove one's own intellectual superiority means being able to talk about everything with great assurance and to drown one's opponent in quotations, facts and name-dropping. Only the French could have been impressed by the conceited gobbledygook of Sartre's *L'être et le néant* (*Being and Nothingness*) which they drooled over for years. Intellectual exclusivism is reinforced by the existence of "les grandes écoles", emergence from whose hallowed halls guarantees great prestige and often a Mafia-like hold on the best jobs. Entrance by stiff competition only, please. Top of the swots are the graduates of Normale Sup, l'ÉNA and l'X.

The ultimate intellectual hothouse is l'École Normale Supérieure where the likes of Sartre, Malraux and de Beauvoir **"ont usé leurs fonds de culottes"** (wore out the seats of their trousers; that is, went to school). The end product is a **"normalien"**, and there ain't nothin' normal about those characters.

Know an **"énarque"**? He/she is a product of the highly competitive, post-graduate École Nationale d'Administration, a super-technocrat with highly developed skills in the art of analysing and dissecting (and not necessarily constructing) with tremendous command of language. He/she is destined for the high ranks of government service, and is a readily identifiable, self-confident character.

What's the X? More reverence, please, l'X being not an unknown quantity but the very selective (intellectually speaking) École Polytechnique for engineering. The English should not be put off by the polytechnic business; this is no second-class institution — one emerges from it with a passport to the upper reaches of the business world, full of theory and perhaps less so of practical knowledge, but that precious piece of paper allows of no querying of one's ability. A **"polytechnicien"** makes a good marriage catch as his earning power is pretty well guaranteed, unlike the aforementioned whose involvement with the meaning of life, art and literature or government service may not necessarily be rewarded in financial terms.

171

Provincial brethren

Leaving Paris, what of the provincial brethren? Beyond the stereotype of the lumpen-provincial, there are regional variations: the "Marseillais" are considered liars and thieves, the "Corses" (Corsicans) lazy loud-mouths, the "Alsaciens" Teutonic "bouffeurs de choucroûte" (sauerkraut-eaters), the "Basques" impetuous, and the "Bretons" thick.

The following commonly used expressions make use of certain accepted images:

faire une promesse de Gascon	to make an empty, vain promise
une histoire marseillaise	a tall story
répondre en normand	to answer evasively, noncommittally
un(e) cousin(e) à la mode de Bretagne	a very distant cousin

A word on the "Normands": inhabitants of a rich, agricultural province noted for its butter, cream and cheese, they are known particularly for their love of rich food. To help ingest gargantuan meals, rather than vomit "à la romaine" they devised "**le trou normand**" (the norman hole): in the middle of a meal, one is given a glass of Calvados, the searing local apple-based spirit whose function is to burn away previously downed dishes, thereby leaving more room — the "hole" in which to shove more food.

XIII

YOUR PH.D. EXAM

Armed with the knowledge gleaned from this book and from
MERDE!, you must surely understand French better and more
deeply than some wanky Ph.D. swot, so I have devised our own
Ph.D. exam. Pass this one and, God forbid, you'll almost be a
Frog! (Answers and translations on pages 87 and 88.)

Part A

"Les citations truquées" (falsified quotes). A few famous quotes
have been tampered with. Where's the joke?

1   Je bande donc je suis. (René Descartes)

2   La faim justifie les moyens. (Friedrich Nietzsche)

3   *Don Diègue*: Rodrigue, as-tu du coeur?

     Rodrigue: Non, j'ai du pique. (Pierre Corneille)

4   L'enfer, c'est les Parigots. (Jean-Paul Sartre)

Part B

Translate:

1   La reine Victoria: j'sais pas si son prince boche, Albert,
était monté comme un âne mais, en tout cas, elle et lui, c'était du
vrai lapinisme! Mais quand son Bébert a passé l'arme à gauche,
elle en a eu gros sur la patate, elle a pleuré comme un veau et
après, le zizi, c'était zéro pour la question. Ça s'appelle l'ère
victorienne: "Le sexe? Nous, on est pas amusés!"

2   L'étranger de Camus est un drôle de zèbre. Sa vieille
claque, il s'en bat l'oeil, il fait avaler son bulletin de naissance à
un bicot; même quand il va se faire raccourcir, il s'en fout du
quart comme du tiers.

3   La Tchécoslovaquie tapait dans l'oeil d'Hitler; il n'y est
pas allé avec le dos de la cuiller, il se l'est payée. Les alliés n'ont
pas remué le petit doigt. Chamberlain est même allé faire du
lèche-cul et est revenu avec la déclaration de Munich qui ne
valait pas un pet de lapin et où Hitler faisait des promesses de
Gascon. Malgré tout, quand il est entré en Pologne, la moutarde
est montée dans le nez des alliés et la guerre fut déclarée.

4   Les Franchouillards ont l'art de faire tout un plat de mecs
désastreux: regardez Louis XIV et Napo, tous deux des mégalos
à caractère de chien. Ils ont ramené leur fraise dans les affaires
des autres pays, mais leurs idées de grandeur ont tourné au
vinaigre. Un type qui s'est bien démerdé quand même c'est cette
girafe de Gaulle, le gégène intello qui, même quand la France
était sur les genoux, a fait des pieds et des mains pour continuer
son one-man-show à Londres.

5   L'URSS mal léché, c'est Kroutchev battant sa table avec sa
godasse.

1   The original is "Je pense donc je suis". But this version shows even greater proof of one's being alive ("bander" = to have an erection).

2   The translation of Nietzsche's "The end justifies the means" uses the French "la fin", but no doubt its homophone "la faim" (hunger) is an equally valid motive for action.

3   This is a classic schooldays joke. In *Le Cid*, the old geezer Don Diègue is slapped across the face by the father of his son's (Rodrigue's) fiancée (Chimène). He thinks it's a big deal and in the scene whence comes the authentic quotation, he is about to ask Rodrigue to kill Chimène's dad and so asks Rodrigue if he's got guts, or balls, or whatever ("as-tu du coeur?"). At school, instead of Corneille's answer, we all used to scream out "Non, j'ai du pique!", a "clever" play on the words for card suits ("du coeur" = hearts, and "du pique" = spades).

4   Sartre thought that hell was other people ("les autres"), but a vision of a hell made up only of Parisians ("Parigots") is terrifying enough.

Part B

1   Queen Victoria: I don't know if her kraut prince, Albert, was well hung, but anyway the pair of them bred like rabbits! But when her Bertie kicked the bucket, she was heartbroken, she cried her eyes out and after that, no more screwing. It's what's called the Victorian era: "Sex? We are not amused!"

2   Camus's outsider is a weirdo. His old mum turns up her toes, he doesn't give a damn, he does in some wog; even when he's going to the guillotine, he couldn't care less.

3   Hitler fancied Czechoslovakia; he wasn't subtle about it, he just treated himself to the place. The allies didn't lift a finger. Chamberlain even went off to do a bit of arse-licking and came back with the Munich declaration which wasn't worth the paper it was written on and in which Hitler made promises he had no intention of keeping. Nonetheless, when he went into Poland, the allies got hot under the collar and war was declared.

4 Froggies love making a big deal out of disastrous guys: take Louis XIV and Boney, both ill-tempered megalomaniacs. They stuck their noses in other countries' business but their grandiose ideas went sour on them. On the other hand, one fellow who managed to do quite well was that beanpole de Gaulle, the intellectual general who, even when France was on her knees, moved heaven and earth to continue his one-man-show in London.

5 "L'URSS mal léché" is a pun on "l'ours mal léché" (= an uncouth fellow; literally a badly licked bear) which applies to the world-famous scene in which Krushchev banged his shoe on a table while making a point at the United Nations.

Latin For Even More Occasions

Henry Beard

The sequel to the highly acclaimed *Latin For All Occasions* is filled with even more essential Latin phrases for all those who share Henry Beard's mission to drag Latin into the twentieth century.

You can impress your friends as never before with your impersonations of Marlon Brando (*'Proeliator fuissem'* – 'I could've been a contender') and James Cagney (*'Tu, rattus turpis!'* – 'You dirty rat!'), breeze by maître d's with confidence (*'Cauponas percenseo'* – 'I'm a restaurant reviewer') and be the life and sole of the office party (*'Estne volumen in toga, an solum tibi libet me videre?'* – 'Is that a scroll in your pocket or are you just pleased to see me?')

Your Latin education simply isn't complete without it.

ISBN 0 00 255134 9